"A genuinely new view of leadership – practical and profound." – Jack Canfield

"Host *brings together many practical leadership strategies to draw people together – effective both in the Board room and on Mount Everest."*

Sir Chris Bonington, mountaineer and author

"Being a great host helps you to be a great networker. This practical book will help you build relationships and engagement both inside and outside your organization."

Dr Ivan Misner, founder, BNI

"A great mix of research, philosophy, stories and insight into what real leadership is about."

Mike Brent, Ashridge Business School

"Having been a host and leader for nearly 40 years, the insights in **Host** *were as refreshingly relevant to me as they will be for any young manager, be they in hospitality or anywhere else where results through others are needed. These easy-to-apply principles will last you a lifetime."*

Philip Newman-Hall, Director/General Manager, Le Manoir aux Quat'Saisons

"Mark and Helen have brought together a range of ideas and stories from across history and the globe into a superbly written and practical primer for today's leaders. The idea of the leader as host may not be a new metaphor but they have set out the many varied and powerful ways that the host/leader can act to bring together people and performance. Key to this is the need for flexibility as exemplified in the stepping forward or stepping back positions and resolving the many paradoxes of leadership. The six roles that the host/leader needs to adopt also add richness to their analysis. But above all it is in the many stories that the reader can truly understand the everyday issues that leaders face and how acting as a host can help them lead effectively. The authors have a down to earth style and convey their ideas with warmth and humour. This is a great addition to the world of leadership ideas and thoroughly recommended regardless of whether you are a CEO or leading a team of one – yourself!"

Ralph Lewis, Chair Greenleaf Centre for Servant-Leadership (UK)

"This fascinating book uses the metaphor of 'hosting' to unravel the complexities of leading and building relationships in organisations and communities. **Host** opens a treasure trove of thoughts, actions, mental maps and advice, all richly illustrated with stories old and new."

Professor John Purcell, Bath University

"Given our modern world with all its problems and all its possibilities isn't it time we re-examined the role of leadership to discover a more useful, natural and easily compelling model? This book says 'yes!' and gives you the insights and tools to do it. The leader as host unleashes powerful new forces for effective goodness that are available naturally to each of us. Buy this book, read this book, you and the world will be glad you did."

Martin Rutte, President of Livelihood & Founder
www.projectheavenonearth.com

"Mark and Helen's book on host leadership provides a fresh new perspective on the need for more and better leadership in organizations. Leadership is no longer a hierarchical notion. It is a requirement among most of the organization. A leader who exhibits the qualities and practices of the leader as host will be setting an example for all those who seek a role model for growing both themselves and the organization."

Alan Kay, author of Fry The Monkeys

"In an already crowded field do we need another book about 'leadership'? Well, yes we do when it is a book like **Host** that seeks to apply leadership thinking to the complex, volatile and ambiguous world in which leaders now operate. Mark McKergow and Helen Bailey have elegantly and practically distilled key concepts about leadership so that they are readily accessible and eminently practical. Fresh, innovative and immediately useable."

John Campbell, Managing Director, Growth Coaching International Pty Ltd

"Leadership and hospitality are about relationships, not transactions. This book brings together a wealth of perspectives, and will energise and refresh anyone looking to build engagement and results in their organisation."

Harry Murray MBE, Chairman, Lucknam Park Hotel & Spa

"I find the concept of leader as host presented in this book to be a very practical and balanced way to think about leadership. **Host** is very helpful in breaking down daunting situations into manageable parts, which then reveals constructive next steps. Indeed, there were a couple of times while reading it where I stopped to perform a small step or send an invitation inspired by the insight gained from the book."

Daniel McCoy, Pixar

"Increasingly modern life leaves people feeling disconnected and distant. When you use the lessons in **Host** to be the most warm, gracious, and effective host your board, team, or clients have ever experienced, the effect will be all the more powerful."

Paul Wicks PhD, TED Fellow and VP of Innovation, PatientsLikeMe

"Leaders of communities and movements, and also of businesses and organisations, have to know when to switch between serving their guests and when to invite them along a new and exciting path. The leader as host is the perfect metaphor for this balancing act, and **Host** is the perfect practical guide on how to do it."

Sanderson Jones, co-founder, Sunday Assembly

"I have followed Mark's work for several years and often reference it during Art of Hosting Conversations that Matter workshops. His metaphor of the leader as host strongly resonates with participants. For those that are practising or developing their relational leadership skills, this book will be a valuable resource for those who are in a host as leader journey."

Jerry Nagel, President, Meadowlark Institute and Art of Hosting Steward

"Incorporating the ideas in this book into my life and leadership has been a deeply satisfying experience. Whether you're hosting gatherings to make your organization more profitable, productive, or innovative, you'll find practical help in this excellent book offered by a couple of first rate minds. Highly recommended!"

Stewart Emery, international best selling co-author of Success Built to Last and Do You Matter?

"Today's world requires a new concept of leadership; one that learns, one that has the gesture of generosity at the level of impulse. Here is the territory, forget the old maps."

Nora Bateson, filmmaker, author, president International Bateson Instititute

Host

Six new ROLES of engagement for teams, organisations, communities and movements

Mark McKergow and Helen Bailey

solutions
books

First published in Great Britain in 2014 by
SolutionsBooks
15 St Georges Avenue
London
N7 0HB
United Kingdom
www.solutionsbooks.com

Rights enquiries should be addressed to: Solutions Books
via info@sfwork.com or by post to the address above

ISBN 978-0-9549749-8-5

Cover design by
Cathi Stevenson

Author photography by
John Cassidy

Design, typesetting and production by
Action Publishing Technology Ltd, Gloucester

Contents

Foreword

By Stephen Josephs, Co-Author of *Leadership Agility*

Has this ever happened to you? It's the end of a day and you're contemplating the problems that demand your attention – fires in operations, unpleasant surprises in a key customer account, complications in relations with your board, a troubling employee survey, and long-term strategic plans that are perpetually on hold. And then it hits you like a bolt of lightning. You push back from your chair and say aloud, "What we need around here is a better metaphor!"

Okay, the last part of the scenario is unlikely—but here's something I can almost guarantee: by the time you are midway through this book, you will have excellent new ideas about how to mobilize the collective intelligence of your teams. And because of how you'll encourage those solutions to arise, your culture will automatically shift towards operating in a more solution-focused, proactive way.

Host invites us to try on a new metaphor for leadership, one that has far-reaching, practical benefits. This unique lens will dramatically add richness and effectiveness to how you execute your role as leader. For many of you, however, that promise may seem only remotely plausible – and with good reason. It begs the question *how could a metaphor, an idea, have that kind of power?*

Without necessarily knowing it, it's likely you already have examples of how metaphors powerfully operate in executives you know. Consider the leader who believes business is war. He thinks of himself as a general and turns to the business of commanding the troops in battle. He will prize *The Art of War* as a business book, just the way *The Prince* by Machiavelli might guide the boardroom maneuvers of those who believe business is a Game of Thrones.

Metaphors not only define our identity; they tell us what's valuable, what's feasible, and what to do next. They exist as mental models, often unexamined and unchallenged by those who live by them. The two metaphors above carry unwanted consequences. What's it like to work for The Commander or Machiavelli? Somewhere in our careers, many of us have learned this firsthand.

McKergow and Bailey call our attention to another metaphor deeply embedded in our business culture: *leader as hero*. Despite leadership-development experts' advice to the contrary, many leaders still operate as though they are the heroes in the unfolding story of their personal and organizational journey.

The authors describe the limitations of that model and how it negatively affects a team's engagement and free flow of ideas. Heroic leaders are also prone to self-importance. Unless it's part of your brand identity (think Miss Piggy and Donald Trump), self-importance is bad for business and for the health of your organization. Yet the hero metaphor survives. We actually *do* need a better metaphor.

Enter Host Leadership. From the C-Suite to small teams, when leaders explore *Host,* they will approach their leadership in a new way, as if they were hosts of a gathering dedicated to achieving benefits for the organization and all its stakeholders. Hosting such a gathering requires that they know and communicate its purpose and direction to its key players. Then the ongoing question becomes how to create the most supportive environment for collective innovation and enthusiasm to arise from the group.

As you read about the six roles of engagement, you will see the authors have given a great deal of thought to how our experience as hosts and guests transfers to leadership challenges. Because they write with such precision about the topic, this slender volume is built for speed. McKergow and Bailey know you're interested in applying concepts as quickly as possible. Indeed, they hit the sweet spot of just enough specificity to guide and inspire.

Albert Einstein said, "Everything should be made as simple as possible, but not simpler." A former physicist himself, McKergow's fondness for simplicity shows up in the elegance of his seminar designs. Participants go from contemplating intriguing ideas to applying and testing them in their specific leadership challenges at work. Similarly, the authors encourage you to work your way through *Host* with a project in mind. That way you can quickly put your ideas to the test.

Helen Bailey complements McKergow's theoretical brilliance with her deep experience in putting these concepts to the test in difficult business situations. Before she dedicated herself to helping businesses achieve their goals through coaching, she was a senior service-quality manager at a leading bank. She has experience in organizations of all sizes, and the illustrations of Host Leadership put into action come largely through her firsthand knowledge of putting them to the test.

McKergow and Bailey have written *Host* with the assumption you want to bring out people's best work, channel your organization's collective intelligence, and deepen your capacity for wise leadership. Furthermore, they believe you want a way to develop your approach to leadership, one that feels like a natural extension of your experience and values. And, because you are busy, you want this wisdom delivered simply, succinctly and memorably in a readable book.

I believe the authors have delivered that book. Now that it's in your hands, you're on the threshold of generating practical ideas you can put into immediate action. I recommend that, after you've taken your ideas for a test drive, you read the book again. You'll get a second infusion of depth and creativity.

Through the authors' website, you'll be able to share your ideas and get the benefit of others' experience. This platform provides you with access to a community of practice with McKergow and Bailey as your masterful and dedicated hosts.

Enjoy!

Stephen Josephs, Ed.D.
Co-Author of *Leadership Agility: Five Levels of Mastery for Anticipating Change*
Author of *Dragons at Work*
Novato, CA

Part One

A New Look at Leadership

1

Time for a New Look at Leadership

"The host is both the first and the last"

~Old Arabic proverb

A host is someone who receives or entertains guests. This is a position with which we are all familiar, at some level. Think about your experience of hosting people in your home or at a celebration. Hosts sometimes have to act heroically – stepping forward, planning, inviting, introducing, providing. They also act in service: stepping back, encouraging, giving space, joining in. The good host can be seen moving effortlessly between them. Hosting has ancient roots and is found across all cultures. We all know good hosting (and good "guesting") at an instinctive gut level.

This book explores the metaphor of host as leader, and leader as host. This timely yet timeless idea is both practical and transformational. It is practical in that the skills, tools and ideas in this book can help us build engagement with people – with individuals and teams at group level, at organizational level (including both corporate and public bodies), and at the wider levels of communities and movements. And it is transformational because, simply by thinking about the leader as a host, we have already opened the door to a rich and wonderful world of awareness, flexibility and history.

We will be looking closely at how modern leaders are already using hosting ideas in practice – sometimes without even knowing it. Former president of South Africa, Nelson Mandela, may have been the most celebrated leader of the second half of the twentieth century. As we will see, he used hosting strategies in many smart ways. We will be looking at examples from him and others, including TED curator Chris Anderson, Everest mountaineer Sir Chris Bonington, and corporate executives, managers and business owners. We have also been exploring what leaders can learn from some of the world's leading hosts, and how hosting customs are inbuilt as part of the world's cultural and spiritual traditions.

The book will help you to:

- Generate engagement and participation to move your organization forward

- Build productive relationships and connections in support of a purposeful endeavor

- Enhance your ability to get results by supporting others

- Increase your awareness of times to act decisively and times to let go

Hosting has always mattered. We think it is time to take a new look at what it means to today's leaders.

What does it mean to lead?

The art of leading was never easy – and it seems to be getting harder all the time. Communication is faster, connection is greater, markets are global, and whatever action we take is part of a great onrushing whirl of conversation and innovation.

In this world, what does it mean to *lead*? People can get all the information they need (apparently from whatever perspective they want) at the touch of a button. They can interact with whomever they want. So, the classical view of a leader as someone who simply issues information and direction is obsolete.

This book offers an alternative. *Leadership* seems to put the focus on the leader. We think this is a mistake. Leading is about a relationship – between the leader and the others. The word *followers* is not a great term for those people, and we will be examining some alternative relationship definitions shortly. It takes two to have a relationship – but the leader is only one person. So this book is about building relationships – at work, in the community, in society, at home – to engage others. This engagement is the key ingredient that leads to increased performance and results.

Leadership as engagement

Some relationships are simply transactional; popping into a convenience store to buy a chocolate bar, for example, usually consists simply of an exchange of one thing for another – chocolate for money. Engagement isn't a big part of this; the fact that both people are there and awake is enough.

In the old days of mass production, everyone had something to do, and as long as they did it, all would be fine; the system would fit together and products would emerge. These kinds of workplaces involved taking engagement out of the equation: one person could easily be replaced by another, and so engagement didn't really matter.

As the twentieth century wore on, it became increasingly clear that engagement was what really counted. If people are engaged – aware, committed, involved, taking action, participating in an ever-changing landscape – they both get more and give more. There is plenty of reliable research on this; the famous "black box" studies led by Professor John Purcell of the University of Bath are a good example.[1] Purcell and his colleagues spent over six years looking at UK companies renowned for their employees' high performance.

Purcell's group found that *even* in organizations with excellent HR policies and practices, and an attractive "big idea" mission that drew people in, the main difference in performance actually came from the relationship between line managers and staff. This was the "black box" that made the difference. Engagement is the key element – without it, everything else is at risk.

Matters are even more stark when organizations and communities are facing *wicked problems* – the boundaries of the problem are uncertain, there are wide-ranging links and connections, and the relationship between cause and effect is not clear: does the chicken or the egg come first? Many of the issues facing organizations and society are becoming increasingly *wicked* – the war on drugs, climate change, developing new business models, global poverty, the banking system, the economy. These are questions which don't easily fit into a single department and have no clear stopping point – a time when it will be all done and dusted.

In such situations, a simple analysis will not yield lasting progress. Engagement is key – getting people together to work on the issues becomes the first priority, rather than expecting an instant answer. British leadership researcher Keith Grint sums it up:

> *"Wicked problems require a transfer of authority from the individual to the collective because only collective engagement can hope to address the problem. The uncertainty involved in wicked problems implies that leadership, as I am defining it, is not a science but an art – the art of engaging a community in facing up to complex collective problems."*[2]

The fact that the world, and consequently the challenges of leadership, is becoming more unpredictable is not in doubt. In the years after 9/11, even the US Army War College, noted for a conservative and hierarchical approach, began to focus on a VUCA future – Volatile, Unpredictable, Complex and Ambiguous.[3] A VUCA world demands agility of response, flexibility to utilize emerging situations, and a mix of clarity (about where we are trying to go) and flexibility in how we get there.

Paradoxes and dilemmas for the modern leader

Leadership has probably always been a paradoxical business. It certainly isn't simple in terms of ascertaining which rules to follow in order to guarantee success. A recent collection of leadership literature[4] came up with the following paradoxes with which leaders have to contend:

- Being wanted and yet also being resisted by their organizations

- Needing to be both *here* as part of the organization and *elsewhere* – apart and somehow separate or different

- Being a member of their group and yet also behaving differently at times – with the consent of the group

- Delivering results, often rapidly, while keeping an eye on long-term developments

- Acting now as well as continuing to follow a journey of development

Work at Ashridge Business School[5] has shown – as if we needed reminding – that leadership is no simple business. Rather than having a straightforward list of behaviors to adopt, leaders are now facing a series of dilemmas – mutually conflicting requirements:

| | **Direction** | |
| Imagining a better future | *while* | keeping focused |

| | **Timing** | |
| Waiting and seeing | *while* | accelerating progress |

| | **Relationships** | |
| Maintaining distance and breadth | *while* | getting close |

| | **Loyalties** | |
| Putting your own needs first | *while* | serving the organization |

| | **Control** | |
| Letting go | *while* | keeping control |

| | **Self-Belief** | |
| Showing vulnerability | *while* | being strong |

| | **Understanding** | |
| Enquiring | *while* | knowing |

This is enough to make anyone's head spin. How on earth are we supposed to do all of this? It feels as if we are being pulled in two opposite directions.

The question is not *which to do* but *when to do each*. This means developing a sense of timing and context – of when to act and when not to act.

Each of the dilemmas listed above comes down in the end to stepping forward or stepping back. Take the first one, for example – direction: keeping focused means stepping forward and ensuring that nothing distracts from the next steps. Imagining a better future, on the other hand, is an activity which requires taking a step back, disengaging from the pressures of everyday work and allowing the imagination to build and create. Similarly, accelerating progress usually means getting in there and exerting pressure, while waiting and seeing is about stepping back and picking the right moment to accelerate, and so on.

Stepping forward and stepping back

In this book, we will be looking in practical detail at the way hosts work, and how this can help us as leaders at all levels to start acting right away in ways that will increase engagement, build performance and bring results. And the very first lesson is that the key question for a host at every moment is:

As a leader, are you going to step forward, or step back?

You're probably thinking that the answer is obvious – leaders step forward! Yes, of course they do – sometimes. The idea of such heroic leadership qualities is thousands of years old. Surely leaders go first, need to be brave, need to build confidence in taking people into the unknown and uncertain future.

We've been looking at how leadership is developing in the twenty-first century, and we are noticing a growing idea that leaders also step *back* sometimes. This needs a different mindset, changing the way we think about the role of the leader from the hero to the engager. There are many reasons for this shift – not least the pace of change, the growth in interconnection and moves towards a knowledge economy, where putting ideas into practice is more important than doing up the same bolt on a machine for thirty years. Modern leaders need to engage others, to encourage them to step forward and act – otherwise, the leader can end up pulling everyone else along, trying to have all the answers and exhausting him/herself in the process.

For some people, stepping back is quite a new idea. We find other leaders who are keen to step back – though they may try it and then struggle with what to do next. Many can't resist the temptation to revert to action and trying to do everything once again.

This idea is not totally new, of course. Bill Walsh was coach of the San Francisco 49ers NFL football team for many years. Bob Johansen interviewed Walsh as part of his VUCA leadership research:

"His biggest challenge as a leader was deciding when to push and when to pull back. So he said he would consciously assess the mood of his organization, and if people were too comfortable, he would create a sense of tension and a sense of urgency. If they were too uptight, he would calm them and pull them back. So that's the kind of delicacy of speed. It's not just running fast all the time. Those that run fast all the time will wear out."[6]

So, stepping back can be good. How would it be if you knew *when* to step back, to invite action and contribution from others, and when to step forward again to nudge, move on or even change direction completely – on a moment-by-moment basis? Wow – that sounds like a *big skill set*, as one of our coaching guru friends put it. Yes, it is – however, the great part is this:

You already know how to do it!

At least in some ways, you already have some awareness and ability from your experience of hosting – whatever that might be – to know when and how to step forward and to step back. In this book, we will share with you the frameworks and ideas that will enable you to develop your skill to an exquisite level of awareness, with many options that you can deploy smoothly at a moment's notice. By learning about and starting to use the six roles and four positions described in this book, you will be building on, tuning and mastering your ability to work with the concept of the leader as a *HOST*.

The leader as host

This is a powerful idea. We all, at some level, know what a host does. We have all invited people around for a meal or a party. We have all been through the balance of preparation and engagement, the joy of introducing people to new friends, the balance of leading, organizing and participating. And we have all been guests too, experiencing the skill of a good host (and perhaps the clumsiness of a bad one) firsthand.

Hosts don't just engage people by drawing them in. They introduce people to each other, make connections and act positively to bring together synergistic groups – people who can complement and add to each other's qualities, skills and interests. The art of arranging – whom to put with whom, what might make an interesting group, even thinking about keeping specific participants apart – is a key element of the host's skill.

Having drawn people together, a good host won't dominate the situation. He/she will flit from one section to another, with a word here and a touch there, keeping an all-encompassing eye on how things are going. But the host won't hog the limelight or become tiresome by constantly taking center stage. The host is always on the lookout for when to intervene and when to leave things ticking along – when to step forward and when to step back. The role of the host transcends and includes both. It entails awareness and timing – and acting instantly.

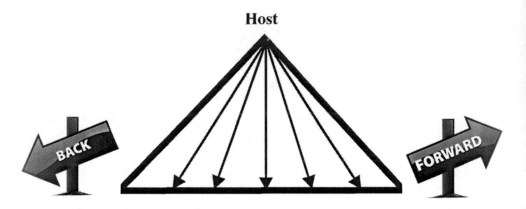

Many people around the world have commented to us that, while the notion of being a *leader* seems like a very big stretch for them, thinking of themselves as a *host* is much easier. This gives us a way in to what can be a very sophisticated and flexible leadership position. Mark first published his view on the dance of the host as leader as long ago as 2009.[7]

We are not alone in being fascinated by the possibilities of leading as hosting. The excellent Art of Hosting movement (www.artofhosting.org) demonstrates ways to build participation in leadership by hosting large-scale conversations that matter. In Sweden, Jan Gunnarsson has been introducing people to Host-manship as welcoming leadership.[8] Margaret Wheatley and colleagues at the Berkana Institute have been using the contrast between hero and host for some time, mainly in a servant-leadership context.[9]

In this book, we seek for the first time to take a deep and detailed look at the role of the host: to show how hosting can inform all kinds of everyday moves – big and small – and how acting as a host is a marvelous way to build engage-ment, relationship and action. We will look at the roots of hospitality, at the different ways it is played out around the world, and take a deep look at what it is to host, and to lead.

The Disraeli Effect

For a first look at what good hosts do, let us turn to leadership guru Warren Bennis, who recounts a story about William Gladstone and Benjamin Disraeli, the famous nineteenth-century British prime ministers:

> *"If you had dinner with William Gladstone, you were left thinking, 'Gladstone is the wittiest, the most intelligent, the most charming person around.' But when you had dinner with Benjamin Disraeli, you were left thinking, 'I'm the wittiest, the most intelligent, the most charming person around!' Gladstone shone but Disraeli created an environment where others could shine. The latter is the more powerful form of leadership, an adventure in which the leader is privileged to find treasure within others and put it to good use."*[10]

Disraeli was clearly the better host. We call this ability to help people see themselves in new and more resourceful ways *the Disraeli effect*. You will find many different ways to engage the Disraeli effect through the coming chapters.

From rules to roles

The term *rules of engagement* is a familiar one to those who have an interest in military history and operations. As well as being the title of a popular US sitcom, rules of engagement are given to troops operating in conflict zones. These rules stipulate precisely under which circumstances force may be used, and to what level. These rules, like all rules, are designed to be followed closely – troops who breach them by using too much force will be in very serious trouble with their own commanders and will bring their operations into disrepute. These rules of engagement are of course about military engagement with the enemy.

Here we are looking at engagement of a different kind – the engagement that draws people in to tackle complex problems, combine their energies and create new futures. In a world in which leaders face constant change and unresolvable dilemmas, hard rules are not going to do the job. Complex and shifting situations require flexible and contextual responses. It's not just about *what to do*; it's *when to do it and when not to do it*.

We are moving the notion of leadership and engagement from an approach that involves *rules* to one that involves *roles*. A role is something you do – at the appropriate time. In the terms of this book, roles are ways of acting and behaving in a social situation. A role is something we slip into and out of all the time – like parent, friend, badminton player. It's nothing to do with acting (like a stage performer). Here, it is about changing our awareness and focus, from day to day, hour to hour, even moment to moment. Now, here's the thing: as a host, we already know how to take on different roles at different times, how to shift from one role to another. We even know when to make the shifts, when to step forward and when to step back again.

The notion of *six roles of a Host Leader* enables us to rapidly build awareness of a wide range of possibilities for action. We can also tap into our inherent knowledge of the dance of the host – forward and back – in each role.

But I'm not a host! What can I do?

The wonderful thing about metaphors is that they can inform our behavior in whatever situation we find ourselves, rather than constraining us into certain contexts. People often say to us, "I inherited my team when I took over the job! How can I be a Host Leader?"

We don't have to be in a hosting position to let hosting inform what we do – to act like a host, and thereby transform relationships around us. Even if the team members were there to begin with, we can start to think of ourselves as the host and the others as guests – and see what happens.

One startling example of this comes from one of the great leaders of the twentieth century, Nelson Mandela. As you probably know, Mandela was an activist for democracy in South Africa, was imprisoned for life by the apartheid regime for treason (for agitating against the state), worked tirelessly from his prison cell to keep the cause alive, was released after twenty-seven years and went on to be the first black president of a new democratic "rainbow nation" in South Africa.

Shortly after he was imprisoned on the feared Robben Island off the coast of Cape Town, Mandela was visited by his (white) lawyer George Bizos. Even under conditions of extreme subjugation, Mandela was able to act like a host. Bizos recalls the meeting:

"On my first visit, in the middle of winter, he was brought to the consulting room where I was waiting. There were eight warders with him, two in front, two at the back, two on each side. Prisoners do not usually set the pace at which they move with their warders. But it was quite obvious that he was – from the open van that they came [in], right up to the little verandah of the consulting rooms. And I stepped down, past the two in front, and embraced him, said, 'Hello.' He returned the greeting [and] immediately asked, 'How's Zami?' which is, how are the children? And he then pulled himself back, and said, 'George, I'm sorry, I have not intro-duced you to my guard of honor.' And then proceeded to introduce each one of the warders by name. Now, the warders were absolutely amazed. I think that this was the first time that they saw a white man and particularly a lawyer, I suppose, coming and embracing a black man, but they were absolutely stunned, and they actually behaved like a guard of honor. They respectfully shook my hand."[11]

Mandela was able to take the lead, even when he was the prisoner surrounded by eight guards. This is the power of the host-guest relationship – it is very deeply ingrained, and we are all so used to it that often we don't notice it happening but simply play our parts. Host Leadership is a way to take a leading position, in a way that draws others in, in a natural way. The details of how you do it will depend on your own culture, your own contexts and your own preferences.

Getting the most out of this book

You will get more from reading this book if you relate it to a real setting. "Host as Leader" is a metaphor, a parallel between two things. By thinking about what we already know about hosting, and what we can learn from excellent hosts around the world, we then view leadership in a new light. This new light will provide a fresh perspective from which we can take action – usually right away – to tackle situations differently and make progress.

The metaphor – described in this book – is the first part of the story. The second part is your own experience. This book is a jumping-off point for expanding and building on that experience. We have done a lot of the work in putting this material together, and we now want you to help us finish your particular copy by connecting the ideas and stories here with your own situation and knowledge.

Some of the ideas in the book will jump right out at you. These may well be the innovations you need right now. Other stories may not quite connect yet. That's fine – perhaps you are already using that strategy, or it may be that you are not yet in a position to use that particular piece. Just move along and discover what else you can enjoy and take inspiration from.

You will find some big ideas here. We often connect them with very everyday examples of small things which can make big differences. These small things are very everyday and mundane, and you may well be tempted to pass them over in search of bigger and bolder strategies. Don't do that – there is a remarkable power in the simple words, the tiny details that bring things to life.

We have added some Reflective Questions at key stages of the book, to help you make your own connections and learning points. It is worth taking a few moments to pause and jot down some initial answers right now. As your role and situation develop, so will your reflections, ideas and actions.

Reflective questions

So, please take a couple of minutes to reflect on these questions, in order to position yourself for a highly productive experience.

- What are the biggest leadership challenges facing you right now?

- What would be the benefits for you of finding new ways to engage people and building increased performance?

- What are the advantages of thinking in terms of flexible roles rather than hard-and-fast rules?

- What was the first thing you liked about the host perspective when you heard about it? What struck you as potentially powerful and useful?

Key points

➢ Leadership in the twenty-first century is about relationships rather than transactions.

➢ Leaders engage people around wicked problems, fast-emerging change and volatile worlds.

➢ Leaders – and hosts – know when to step forward and back.

➢ Host Leadership is about roles, not rules – roles that we take on for a while, rather than rules we always follow.

➢ Anyone can think like a host – even when the situation looks very unpromising.

Did you know you can get free bonus resources on Host Leadership from www.hostleadership.com? Use the code you'll find at the end of the last chapter to sign in.

2

Hosting: A New Yet Ancient Metaphor

"...Good company, good wine, good welcome, can make good people."

~Sir Henry Guildford in Henry VIII (William Shakespeare)

We begin our look at the ideas of hosting with a look at the history and significance of the role of the host. This chapter will help expand our thinking about what it means to be a host, and how that role is pivotal in building communities and cultures around the world.

In the modern world, we usually think of hosting as either about inviting family, friends or colleagues around for a party or meal, or as something done by (frequently cheesy and cheery) game-show hosts on TV. The hospitality "industry" is a huge sector of the economy, with hotels, restaurants, guest houses, pubs, conference centers, convention halls and even disused churches vying to hold our gatherings and functions. However, it wasn't always this way.

Ancient origins

The *Oxford English Dictionary* gives the origin of the English word host as coming from the Indo-European word *ghosti* – from which stem both host and guest. Even in ancient times, these two concepts were intimately bound together. The idea appears in ancient Greek as *xenia* (from which we get the unfortunately oft-used word xenophobia, a fear of strangers), and in Latin as *hospes*. This turns into the Old French word *hoste*, which in French becomes *hôte*, from where we get *hotel*. If you've ever been offered a "*table d'hôte*" menu in Europe, it means literally the table of the host – a set menu consisting of what the host would be eating, which they have invited you to share. *Hospes* also gives us many other words connected to hosting – hospitality, hospitable and also hospital – originally in the middle ages a place where people were welcomed and cared for when they were sick. There not being much in the way of medicine in those days, the care aspect was by far the biggest part of the treatment.

The ancient ways of hosting can still be seen in traditional cultures. The Bedouin peoples of the desert still maintain a strict code of hospitality. If you meet a stranger, you must invite him in and offer him tea and refreshment, without thought of who he is or where he comes from. This is a very practical arrangement – the resident people are obliged to protect and help travelers in a hostile environment. In the days before telephones and Holiday Inn Express, this was the only kind of shelter to be found in the harsh desert climate, and only these traditions made it possible to move around without a significant chance of perishing.

This kind of hospitality is still practiced in remote areas of the world today. Tim Cope, author of *On The Trail of Genghis Khan*, traveled the Mongolian steppes first on a bicycle and then on horseback. He was amazed at the capacity of the indigenous people to move around, carrying their homes with total freedom. He recalls:

> *"Hospitality is the lynchpin of survival on the steppe. In the desert in Kazakhstan it was reaching 50C outside during the day, it's an environment with no trees for thousands of miles, not much water, I had to ride by night and then find somewhere to shelter – it was a matter of life and death. These people with no obligation to me took me into their underground huts, I'd be wined and dined on fermented camel's milk, sometimes the charred head of a horse [a rare delicacy in those parts] if I was lucky – they took me in like their long-lost son."*[1]

Hosting around the world: A host of meanings

There are other very different meanings of the word host, from different roots. A multitude or great number can be called a host, from the Latin *hostis*, originally meaning enemy, and used in connection with a large army. This root also gives us the modern word hostile. In the early seventeenth century, the use of this word shifted from armies to large numbers, such as the "heavenly host" of angels in the Christian tradition. Christians also use the word host to mean the consecrated bread taken in the communion ceremony, which comes from yet another Latin word, *hostia*, meaning victim or sacrifice. In the Christian meaning, this is Christ, of course, but the word also gives us the modern term hostage, someone who is kept as security and (presumably) as a potential sacrifice. These three Latin words, hospes, hostis and hostia, are probably all related in the mists of time.

The idea of hosting and hospitality is an important element of every cultural and spiritual tradition. We will be seeing examples from different places throughout this book. Hosting is truly an international, intercultural and inter-denominational concept. It is also inter-gender – many of the aspects of hosting include feminine elements as well as masculine, maintaining a key role without being subservient.

Abraham and the three visitors

This story is very old indeed – a foundational tale for the monotheistic faiths of Christianity, Judaism and Islam. By that route, it has become folded into the fabric of many of the world's societies and cultures. Abraham is sitting at the entrance to his tent in the heat of the day, near the great trees of Mamre. As the story is told, Abraham looks up and sees three men standing nearby. He hurries to meet them, bows low to the ground and invites them to come and rest under a tree while water is brought to wash their feet and they can be given something to eat. The three strangers accept. Abraham then hurries into the tent, asks his wife Sarah to prepare bread, selects a choice calf to provide meat to be prepared urgently by a servant, then bring curds, milk and the prepared calf to the strangers. While they eat, Abraham waits nearby under the tree.[2] The three strangers turn out to be angels, who reveal that Abraham's wife Sarah is to have a child the following year, which seems strange given her advanced years. Nonetheless, Abraham's son Isaac is indeed born within the year.

This story is one of hosting in the ancient sense – Abraham sees strangers in the heat of the day, and leaps into action to welcome them into his tent. The moral is clear – welcome people, and they can turn out to bring you great gifts. In the text, Abraham describes himself as their servant – and indeed while they are there, he serves them. But he is not a "servant" in the indentured sense, a retainer owned by the travelers. He is much more a host, who very actively notices the needs of others and seeks to fulfill them as best he can by inviting them in. He steps forward and invites the strangers into his tent. He then actively seeks to prepare food and drink. This *initiating* part of hosting will be very important in our discussion of Host Leadership later on. Then, having sat the guests down, he steps back and stands near them under the tree, keeping an eye on how things are going and ready to step forward again when needed – either because one of his guests wants something, or because he has seen something that he must deal with.

We include this story here as a founding tale of society. To welcome and sustain people is a key role in community and life – and often the guests will bring much more than the host expected. We will return to this idea of welcoming guests later in this chapter.

What is a host?

Now let's start to look at how these origins might have survived into an understanding of hosting today. We will begin with a definition.

The Oxford English Dictionary gives the following main definition:

"Host (n.) a person who receives or entertains guests"

These guests may be there by long-standing arrangement and invitation, or they may have just shown up out of the blue. They may be old friends or they may be total strangers. Whatever the situation, *host* is defined relationally – it makes no sense to talk about hosts unless there are also guests in the picture. The same can be said about leadership, of course – much is being made in modern leadership writing about the lack of attention given to *followers*. Increasingly, attempts are being made to find a better word than *follower*, which seems rather sheep-like in a world looking for empowered and active people. To think of the *other* as a guest takes us into a whole new domain of thinking and acting.

Leadership metaphors and relationships

We have already seen how the relationship between host and guest is a mutually co-defining one. It makes little sense to speak of being a host if there are not guests, and none in prospect. We are starting to see how the host steps forward and back, both initiating events and supporting the guests.

This sense of relationship gives a good way to look at two other metaphors for leadership: leader as hero and leader as servant. What is the relationship implied by these metaphors?

The hero: to the rescue

The idea of a leader as a heroic figure is deeply engrained in our society. Powerful men (usually), fast acting, all-knowing, saving the situation, turning things around, avoiding disaster. This is a caricature, but images like the Lone Ranger, Lee Iacocca (Chrysler) and Joan of Arc spring to mind. There are related archetypes in the leadership literature – the king and the warrior are two based on the work of Jung; the shepherd has ancient Biblical roots. In each case the leader can be relied upon in times of trouble to pull things through.

Harvard Business School leadership writer Sharon Daloz Parks sums up the situation very nicely:

> *"It has become almost a cliché among leadership theorists to disavow a heroic command-and-control model of leadership. But the heroic image of leadership that prevails in the conventional mind is more than a model. It is a deep and abiding myth."*[3]

The survival of this myth in the public imagination is perhaps the most telling thing. It seems that we need some kind of person to resort to in difficult times. In tough times, we long for a hero to come along – someone in whom we can place our trust, who inspires confidence, who will save the day. Yet with the postmodern world of ever greater connectedness, multiple perspectives and wicked problems, the commanding-and-controlling hero has never looked more out of place.

The difficulty with the hero leader myth can be seen most starkly in terms of the implied relationship with the followers. The counterpart of hero is *rescued*. In simple terms, heroes don't ask; they tell. Followers, if they know what's good, will do what the hero says – if they don't, they will have spoilt the effect. In our terms, heroes step forward – and forward. This is not at all what's wanted in organizations that seek to engage people's skills, talents and creativity. This not-so-useful relationship plays out in several unfortunate ways:

1. The hero leader is seen as all-knowing and the followers all-dependent; the people cannot rescue themselves but rely on the appearance of the hero.

2. The illusion of control – by being all-knowing and strong and brave, leaders can avert disaster by their own efforts alone. The interdependent and complex world is not so amenable to this outlook.

3. The homogeneous imagery of the followers – kings have subjects, shepherds have flocks of sheep. This seems to suggest homogeneity among the masses. All the followers are the same and therefore can be thought of as one (rather than individuals).

4. The willingness of the hero (warrior, king, even shepherd) to die in the act of rescue – it is their duty to risk being destroyed or to destroy (actually or metaphorically).

There have been various attempts over the years to produce alternatives to the hero leader. Bill Joiner and Stephen Josephs, in their book *Leadership Agility*,[4] point out the distinction between heroic and post-heroic leadership. Heroic leaders succeed because of their expertise (in the task they are leading) and/or their effort, energy and achievement. They know more, they work longer, they work harder. In the heroic view, it's all about *ME* (the leader) – they couldn't do it if I wasn't here.

In Joiner and Josephs' model, the expert and achiever leadership styles are viewed as stages through which leaders go on their developmental journey. However, many don't get past this stage – some ninety percent of leaders in corporate America are estimated to be operating from this position.

The good news, though, is that help is at hand. It is quite feasible to learn and develop our skills to move beyond the hero position. A key difference when it comes to helping people make this transition is that it's not about *ME* anymore; it's much more about *US* – getting results through engaging others, building cooperation, enhancing relationships and pulling together so that the energies and experience of all are fully engaged.

The servant: looking after the master

There is clearly more to leadership than heroism. But what? One key countering idea is that of Servant-Leadership, proposed by Robert K Greenleaf in the 1970s and subsequently taken up by many management thinkers.

Inspired by the Herman Hesse novella *The Journey to the East*, Greenleaf arrived at the conclusion that great leaders must first serve others – and this fact is what shows their true greatness. The story concerns a group making a spiritual journey. They are accompanied by Leo, a servant who looks after the group, eases the way and cares for them. The journey goes well until Leo disappears, whereupon the party begins to fall apart – they cannot cope without him and the journey has to be abandoned. Many years later, the narrator finally stumbles across Leo and is taken to the religious order which originally sponsored the journey. There he discovers that Leo is in fact the head of the order – its guiding spirit.

This idea is a brilliant counterblast to the hero leader. It has become influential in many fields and has been a catalyst for later thinking about spiritual practice and its connection and function in leadership. It brings to the fore the leader's need to respond to their followers and sustain the community, to steward it and hold it in trust for future generations. Servant-Leadership has been most influential in places with a sophisticated view of service, such as church organizations. We wish it were more widely used (as well as widely spoken about).

Again, some of the difficulties of Servant-Leadership can be seen when we consider the counterpart – the master. Placing the followers in the position of "master" is, of course, a counterintuitive and paradoxical move. It helps us to think about the purpose of the leader in terms of supporting the organization, drawing authority from the organization, acting in service. However, we fear that the accountabilities of this relationship are not clear, particularly to modern eyes.

In the twenty-first century, most of us are long separated from the everyday idea of servants – we tend to think instinctively of something like a waiter, whose job is simply to do our bidding, one who steps back until ordered otherwise. In history and literature, the master/servant relationship is a rich and multidimensional one – think of Jeeves and Wooster, Leporello and Don Giovanni, Sancho Panza and Don Quixote, even Carson the butler and Lord Grantham in TV's *Downton Abbey*. In these relationships, the servant is often better informed than the master, and uses his/her wits and influence to help in difficult times, while carefully maintaining the overall idea that the master is (naturally) "in charge."

In modern times, most people don't have servants, and therefore are not at all familiar with the richness and complexity of these relationships, which means that the metaphor of servant as leader is less potent than it might once have been. Many people view the servant as being at the whim/mercy of the master. There are apparent difficulties with responsibility – if the master wants to go a certain way, how accountable is the servant? This tension is of course part of a full treatment in Servant-Leadership and provides much richness, if the student can be persuaded to persevere. It is also interesting to note that in the Hesse story mentioned above, the group does not realize that their servant has been playing a leadership role until it is too late – which of course works well in terms of a parable but not so well in terms of a leadership practice.

The image of servant is also not a compelling one to those (for example, women and ethnic minorities) who are traditionally cast in such a role; they would prefer a new image to move towards. Supporters of Servant-Leadership make the point that detailed study can show new ways to view the role, but this is perhaps unlikely if the initial image does not appeal.

The host: receiving guests

The host-guest relationship, as we have seen, is as ancient as humanity. Hosts often take a lead, initiating and inviting. The guests have their part to play as well – to respect the host's space, not to put their feet on the furniture, not to steal the teaspoons. This bond of reciprocity appears as a mutual, but not equal, relationship. The host has responsibility for the guests. The guests, for their part, are culturally expected not to abuse or take advantage of their host. In some Bedouin cultures, guests – even enemies – may expect hospitality for up to three days. During this time, they receive full protection from the hosting clan. (After this time, there are various ways for the host to show the guests it's time to leave – with increasing forcefulness.)

If heroes step forward and servants step back, then the host does both. The key to good hosting, and to good Host Leadership, is not simply in the flexibility of being able to move from one to the other, but in the awareness and timing of when to do so. Host Leaders initiate and step forward – like Abraham outside his tent. They may then step back while their guests enjoy the hospitality, the space, and the resources offered, but are always ready to step forward again, either to move things along in a timely way, or to respond to an emergency or crisis.

Hosting should be forthcoming and generous – but it can also be important not to over-step what is required or expected. In Japan there is even a word, *omotenashi*, for the spirit of good hospitality. One part of omotenashi is the importance of a non-dominant relationship between the person offering hospitality and the person receiving it. Hosting can involve anticipating what might be needed, and delivering it unobtrusively. Maintaining this balance in Japan also means not exceeding the expectations of your guests by *too* much.

A little higher than expected is great. A lot higher than expected means that the expectations may have been set mistakenly, which reflects poorly on the host.

Hosting around the world: Murder in the moonlight

Transgressing the bond of hospitality was historically a very serious business. One well-known example from history is the Massacre of Glencoe in Scotland. On February 12, 1692, thirty-eight members of the Clan MacDonald of Glencoe were killed by soldiers under the command of Captain Robert Campbell of Glenlyon, ostensibly for being slow to pledge allegiance to the new monarchs William and Mary. Another forty women and children are said to have died of exposure in the cold Scottish winter after their homes were burned.

What made this awful crime even more heinous was that Campbell's troops were guests of the MacDonalds – they had arrived some days earlier and been offered hospitality. Under the Scots law of the time, this was "murder under trust," a special category of crime. The massacre resulted in centuries of enmity between the MacDonalds and the Campbells, which is still felt even today. The transgressing of hospitality also appears in Shakespeare – Macbeth breaks the tradition of hosting by murdering King Duncan while Duncan is his guest, thus destroying the natural order of things. In which modern situations might we step very carefully, so as not to create a rift lasting generations?

The art of hosting is a very relational one. We are very keen on the ideas of relationships as being constructed in conversation, and so the precise details of how a Host Leader engages with their guests will make a big difference. We will be seeing many examples of this throughout the book. There is a lot of scholarship appearing about the linguistic aspects of inviting people into relationship – see, for example, Lone Hersted and Kenneth Gergen's excellent book *Relational Leading*.[5]

We are aiming to keep this book practical and so won't be making many specific references to this "relational" way of thinking in the book – in the same way that a book on football doesn't need to keep referring to gravity and the tendency for things to fall to earth when not otherwise held up. It's there; it makes whatever difference it makes. What we are seeking to do is to engage your knowledge, skill and awareness in making progress in the world, including gravity, social construction and everything else.

For our purposes in this book, we can start from this definition:

> Host Leader (n.) someone who engages fellow participants in a purposeful endeavor

This will include doing all the things that hosts do – inviting, welcoming into a space, supporting, being open to possibility, and sharing responsibility.

Welcome to the idea of Host Leadership. Let's now take a first look at how this new yet ancient metaphor might open up our thinking as leaders today – blending the old and the new.

Welcoming – a big chance for openness and connection

Hosting and welcoming go hand in hand. This may seem a little obvious; however, even the simple act of answering the door can offer an opportunity for significant interaction and connection.

We've seen how hospitality is a key strand of many spiritual traditions. One notable strand comes from the Benedictines. Fifteen hundred years ago, St Benedict of Nursia laid down rules for monks living in community under the authority of an abbot. These rules have survived as the guiding principles for Benedictine communities and in similar forms for other orders, including female convents, which can easily be found online.[6]

The first Benedictine communities were in the desert regions of the Holy Land, and so the hospitality culture of the nomads is also a part of the Rule of St Benedict. In those days, much like today, monasteries were rather private places dedicated to prayer, study, reflection and work. This might translate into a wariness of visitors and a reluctance to engage with the wider populace, but St Benedict was clearly alive to the possibility for exchange, and included a specific section on how the monks were to treat guests – in particular unexpected guests, there being no easy ways to communicate in advance that one was arriving.

Chapter 53 of the Rule, "On the receptions of guests," opens in the boldest possible way: *"Let all guests who arrive be received as Christ, because He will say: 'I was a stranger and you took Me in.'"*

Let all guests be received as Christ! The highest possible honor and gladness is to be shown to *all* guests. In the Christian tradition, followers live in the hope and expectation of the return of the Messiah, and it is thought that when He comes again it will not be dripping in gold and garlanded with flowers, but rather as a poor, bedraggled stranger. We don't expect he will turn up in a smart suit with a business card that reads "The Messiah." A key strand of the Christian tradition, as with the other monotheistic faiths Judaism and Islam, is therefore to be open and welcoming to strangers. Benedict sets this out in the strongest terms, and lets no one be in any doubt of the greeting to be shown. The rule continues:

"In the greeting let all humility be shown to the guests, whether coming or going; with the head bowed down or the whole body prostrate on the ground, let Christ be adored in them as He is also received."

While we are not suggesting that lying prostrate is appropriate in today's circumstances, this passage shows clearly how a sense of humility and honor is a key part of hosting in this tradition. This all seems a very long way from mechanically clicking on the "friend" button in Facebook requests!

The value of humility in leadership is not, of course, restricted to the Christian tradition. Crazy Horse, the great Lakota leader who defeated Lieutenant Colonel George Custer's 7th Cavalry at the Battle of the Little Bighorn in 1876, came from a long tradition of leadership, described by Joseph M. Marshall III in *The Lakota Way:*[7]

"Humility was a virtue that the Lakota of old expected their leaders to possess. A quiet, humble person, we believed, was aware of other people and other things. An arrogant, boastful man was only aware of himself. … Humility can provide clarity, where arrogance makes a cloud. A humble person rarely stumbles, the old ones say, because such a person walks with face toward the Earth and can see the path ahead … The burden of humility is light because a truly humble person divests himself or herself of the need for recognition."

Meeting with possibility

These ancient traditions already point towards an important element of Host Leadership – meeting with possibility. If we meet people with a mindset that we already know about them and the relationship we have with them, then that's how things will continue to be. However, if we meet people anew – as someone endowed with rich and as-yet-unknown possibilities – then the door is open for new joint discoveries. In the world of management, a "meeting" is usually a tightly choreographed affair of agendas, minutes, decisions and actions. While this is one part of running an efficient organization, the Host Leader will also be aware of the value of more open encounters.

As an interesting thought, we invite you to meet the ideas in the rest of this book with possibility.

Hosting around the world: Reunión or encuentro?

In the Spanish language, there are two words for meeting. A meeting of a committee or some such is called a reunión – literally, a *reunion* of people who have met before. This will be an agendas-to-actions kind of business meeting. However, there is another word – encuentro – for a chance meeting, without the burden of objectives and expectations. Host Leaders know the benefits of being open, welcoming and engaging in meeting people, to discover new connections rather than merely reconfirming their initial prejudices and expectations. When is your next chance to have a meeting on the basis of encuentro, rather than reunión?

It's time to look at a key question in our quest for a rich and workable view of leadership: what do hosts actually do? This is the topic of our next chapter.

Reflective questions

• How has your view of hosting been expanded by this chapter?

• How can the host/guest relationship be applied in your context – who are your "guests?" Think inside and outside your organization.

• Where might you have opportunities for more openness and connection?

• When would it be useful to meet with more possibility and less certainty – an *encuentro* rather than a *reunión*?

Key points

➢ Hosting and hospitality are very ancient aspects of human cultures and societies.

➢ The word *host* comes from the same word origins as *guest, hospitable* and *hospital*.

➢ Leadership metaphors imply a relationship with the others. These can help us to understand the meaning and implications of each metaphor.

  • Hero and rescued
  • Servant and master
  • Host and guest

➢ Host Leaders are active in welcoming guests and strangers with openness to resources and possibility.

3

What Do Hosts Do?

> *"Hospitality means primarily the creation of free space where the stranger can enter and become a friend instead of an enemy. Hospitality is not to change people, but to offer them space where change can take place."*
>
> ~Henri Nouwen, Reaching Out

In the previous chapter, we looked at hosting in terms of relationships and the big picture of how hosting has developed through the ages. In this chapter, we want to look more concretely at what hosts do. There are many cultural variations around the world, of course, and we will be looking at those throughout the book – as you are seeing in the *Hosting around the world* boxes. There are some basics, however, that seem to be universal.

The first question at all times for a Host Leader is: *Should I step forward or step back?*

We see Host Leadership as a dance. Good hosts know how and when to step forward – and make a positive and definite move to help things along, and when to step back – to create a space for others to act and interact. Most leadership writing is concerned with stepping forward and acting. We  believe, however, that knowing when NOT to act is also a key element, and one that is made very  clear by the hosting metaphor. Over the following chapters, we will explore what it means to step forward and back, and to increase our skill levels until the moves become natural and instinctive.

The flexibility of acting, observing, reflecting and acting again in rapid succession, with continuing awareness and options, is both a way to host and a way to make progress in a world which is changing and shifting constantly. We will examine the implications of such a world view in the forthcoming *User's Guide to the Future* chapter.

We will be using this chapter to introduce our six roles of a Host Leader. These roles have emerged from over a decade of research, thinking and experimentation. They offer a comprehensive yet flexible way to think about our actions, options and choices in real-life situations, without oversimplifying or artificially reducing the richness and complexity of the world around us.

Alongside this, we will also introduce our four positions for a Host Leader. These show the places we can take up, relative to our "guests," to act, observe, reflect and participate. The four positions add some great flexibility and variety to this basic question and, together with the six roles, bring a world of responsiveness and inclusion to our fingertips.

We will also be dealing with some of the key questions we are often asked when we speak on Host Leadership around the world. People love the metaphor, and there are some questions which come up regularly too. We'll be examining those before getting into the details of the positions and roles in subsequent chapters.

What do we do, as hosts?

At a high level, we might look at hosting as being about setting context, giving protection and enabling community. Hosts are usually the ones who step forward with an idea, an offer or a possibility. A host is always a context setter – providing an environment or space into which others will come. The others may be invited to change the space and participate in it, but the host is the first to have the opportunity to set things up. This is a very powerful position when used with skill – for example, governments are always keen to host summit meetings or talks, as they know that there will be opportunities to influence discussions in ways which are simply not open to the other participants.

Hosts offer protection – at some level – in that they take some of the responsibility for providing shelter, food, and warmth. As we saw earlier, hosts have a duty to protect their guests (even if the threat nowadays is generally much less than it was in Shakespeare's time). Even in dangerous situations, however, the armed forces still hold fast the importance of officers providing for the troops in their charge.

Hosts enable community – by gathering people under one roof, they bring them together, help them face troubles jointly rather than separately, and draw on each other for skills, strengths, and support.

And above all, hosts are fluid and flexible in their work and attention. They are continually stepping forward and back, nudging where needed and letting things flow. Our six roles are a way to learn to focus our attention on what might need to be done next, do something and then step back and look again.

Hosting around the world: The joy of the Saxon mead hall

Over a thousand years ago, the peoples of the British Isles and northern European world lived a tough and rugged life. Dangers abounded, raiders were a constant threat, and forming alliances was a vital feature of society. Epic poems such as *Beowulf* and the Icelandic sagas show that the key hub, the safest place, was the mead hall.

From the fifth century into early medieval times, each lord had a hall, a large building (by the standards of the time) where songs were sung, celebrations held, anniversaries marked, guests entertained, battles planned and oaths of allegiance sworn. The lord and his retainers would also live there. The mead hall was a place of feasting, boasting and community – all under-pinned by mead (the honey-based alcoholic drink of the time) and good food. The mead hall was also a place of safety, where the lord's protection was strongest, and a place of reconciliation after conflict.

The literature of the time is full of references to "hall joys," the exultant feeling of being safe with friends, warm and well fed. In *Beowulf*, the rebuilding of the mead hall symbolizes the rebirth of the community. The missionary Paulinus, preaching to King Edwin of Northumbria, noticed a bird fly into, across and out of the mead hall and used this image to convey the magic of this life we are gifted (in the company of others), in contrast to the coldness and uncertainty before and the mystery of what may come after, showing the centrality of the mead hall's fellowship to life itself.[1]

What place do you have which might be used as a mead hall? Supposing you had one, what would you do and who would you like to entertain?

Hosting in practice: six roles

We might start to think first about the roles of host and guest in connection with a very concrete everyday example from the more modern period of hosting, in which guests are invited to a planned event like a party. This is an everyday example from social life, to explore the metaphor. Later we will link these ideas to work and organizational settings.

In advance

The host somehow comes to a decision that a party would be a good idea. They will be aware of what else is happening, who they'd like to see, and what the constraints might be in terms of space, weather, people's work and so on. This looks like a decision, but actually it is preceded by a period of *listening* – hearing what is there, what is not yet there, and what would be their hopes and intentions for acting. They then decide to begin the planning.

This is the role of the *Initiator* in Host Leadership. Initiators are very aware of what is needed and then spring into action with both an idea of what might be, and some small next steps. Stepping back in awareness and readiness to act, and then stepping forward into action, are both fundamentals for the host.

The host decides to hold a party, what kind of party, where and when, and makes plans. They then decide which guests to invite, and invites them. This is the *Inviter* role in action. Inviting is connected strongly with soft power and influence, the outstretched hand of welcome. Stepping forward to invite is coupled with stepping back to offer choice for the guests – to accept or not. This space and choice is what helps to produce commitment and involvement for those invited.

The host then procures food, drink and any entertainments to be laid on. They choose and prepare the space carefully, in support of their hopes. The host is acting as *Space Creator* here, making active choices and plans, and in some ways is acting rather heroically by deciding what they want and laying the ground to make it happen. One thing hosts can often do is to prepare actively for what they hope and intend will happen – in the knowledge that once things get going, emergence will take over and the unexpected will often make an appearance.

During the party

Now that the party is underway, the host's role changes dramatically. The host is usually to be found answering the door and welcoming the guests over the threshold.

This is part of the *Gatekeeper* role, deciding in all kinds of ways what is to be encouraged and what is to be discouraged. This links back to the invitation stage, where the guests have already had some hints about what to expect and what is expected of them in turn. It is part of the host's duty to make some choices about their event, and how to handle what emerges. One never knows what might happen – be it a dropped jar of beetroot on a fine white shirt, the failure of the soufflé, or even the arrival of unwelcome gatecrashers. The guests will tend to look first to the host, who may be required to quickly move in these cases from something like a serving position to a more heroic lead – or not – in protecting the boundaries of the party. It all depends on the kind of event that has transpired (which may or may not be as the host intended).

Once the guests are welcomed, the host will often make introductions, connecting the guests to each other, and seeing that everyone is suitably involved and engaged. This is the *Connector* role. Note that this *does not* mean hogging the limelight or leading every conversation. It *does* mean taking care that everyone is attended to, making people aware of transitions (like moving from drinks to dinner), seeing that no one is left out and so on. They must respond to their guests – no event like that can be choreographed entirely. In this way they are perhaps acting more like servants.

And, of course, the host joins in with their guests – they eat the same food and are mostly in the same room. This is not like the role of the servant, who would be expected to eat out of sight at some other time. The host is then a *Co-Participator* with their guests, stepping forward to lead the way and then stepping back to allow others to be served first. Hosts, and leaders, eat last (as Simon Sinek has pointed out).[2]

Afterwards

At the end of the event, the host says goodbye to the guests and in all probability is left, as the Space Creator, to do the cleaning up. Once again, they combine elements of heroism with elements of serving. This act of being "the last" as well as "the first" is characteristic of Host Leaders – for example, the captain of a sinking ship must see that everyone else is safe before they themselves leave. This will again involve the role of Gatekeeper – seeing everyone out is as much a part of the host's role as welcoming them. There may be more Connecting to be done in the light of what has happened, linking the new people we've met with others. Finally, the Initiator role will appear again as the host thinks of their next event, how it could be better and what new calls to action may be emerging on the horizon.

This is a concrete and everyday example – but it can already provoke our thinking on leadership and how we practice it. As we go on to explore the rich history (*hostory*?) of the role, we will find that it not only appears in every society, and that it forms a very deep and often spiritual connection between people.

Four positions for a Host Leader

Our investigation of hosting has also led us to the idea that a key thing hosts do is spend time in four distinct *positions*. A host or Host Leader adopts these positions as they engage with people and events. These are, very briefly:

In the spotlight – Being the focus of attention, out front, making things happen

With the guests – Still in view of everyone, but being "one of the group" – not the overall center of attention

In the gallery – Standing back, taking an overview of what's happening (like Abraham under his tree)

In the kitchen – In a more private and intimate space, preparing and reflecting

Again, a Host Leader will know the value of all these positions and will be able to move from one to another as events unfold. We will be looking at the roles and positions in detail in the next chapters of this book.

Hosting around the world: Hausrecht *in Germany*

The host holds a natural authority within their own space. This is true the world over – the authority is both culturally accepted and is earned by giving attention and care to the guests, who then want to reciprocate in cooperation. In Germany, there is even a word for the responsibility of the host – *Hausrecht*. This literally translates as "house rights." For example, they decide who gets to come; they can throw people out. Nobody else at the party can make that decision. While people's idea of hosting is evolving in the twenty-first century, it will inevitably be based on these older ideas. How are you letting people know about your own *Hausrecht* and expectations?

Using the six roles and four positions

As this book unfolds, we will be examining the six roles and four positions of a Host Leader. As we do so, remember the distinction between a *rule* and a *role*. Rules must be followed all the time. Roles are for stepping into and out of, for adopting when the need arises.

When we are facing leadership challenges, or are just thinking about what to do next, we can use the roles and positions as a kind of buffet menu. Out of all the choices, what seems the most useful next focus? The key questions to ask are therefore:

•   **Am I going to step forward or step back (next)?**

•   **In which role? (what am I going to do?)**

•   **And in which position? (where am I going to do it?)**

We can then use the six roles to decide on some very small next steps, put these into action, and respond and build on the subsequent emerging events. This is not about planning the whole journey; it is about having an idea of the destination and then setting out with the first steps. We will consider this "agile" philosophy in the *User's Guide to the Future* in Chapter 4.

The six roles and four positions offer a sophisticated new view of leadership activities and thinking. We will be using these terms throughout the book to build a language, as well as a framework, to help guide and navigate through the inevitable twists and turns of life.

Host: roles and positions
Am I going to step forward, or step back?
In which role & in which position?

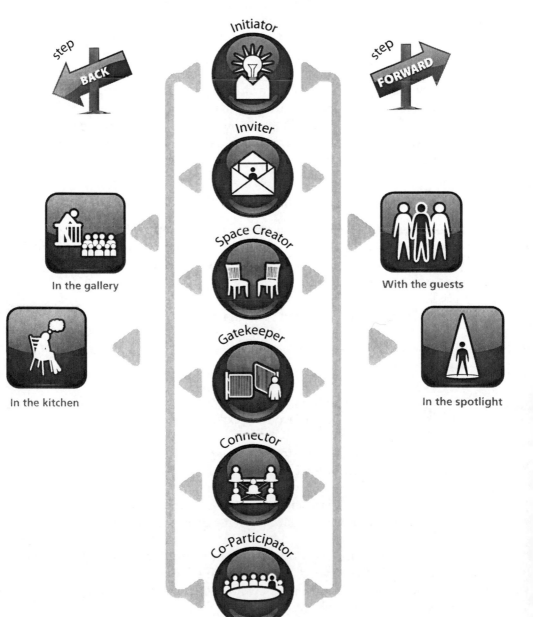

If you are feeling keen to try out this process right now on a pressing situation, then turn to Chapter 12, where you can find a punchy summary of the roles and positions, and some examples of putting them into action. Then you could turn back to here, to continue to explore the details of hosting, leadership and engagement.

Common questions about leading as a host

We find that many people around the world find the metaphor of the leader as host to be an instantly appealing one. They then look at us as if to say, "Aha! But what about…?" You may be thinking of some of these questions right now, so let us give some initial answers and thoughts which may help you set aside whatever initial concerns you may have.

Can I use Host Leadership at any level of an organization?

We are often asked about how Host Leadership can apply within an organization. Can there only be one host? Of course not. We think that the principles and practices of Host Leadership can be applied at all levels within an organization and beyond.

- If you are leading a group, then you can be a Host Leader

- If you are leading a temporary group like a project team, you can be a Host Leader

- If you are working with others, you can be a Host Leader and start to use the six roles to enhance your working experience

- If you are working with customers and/or suppliers, you can be a Host Leader and host their interactions with you and your organization

- If you are working with patients, learners or other kinds of service user, you can be a Host Leader with regard to their experiences with you

Within an organization, it's very common to find Host Leaders who are hosting their teams and also being good "guests" within wider teams of which they are members. Good Host Leaders also know how to be good guests and play great roles as team players and effective participants and contributors.

Is this idea too simple?

The beauty of a metaphor is that it conveys a great deal in just a few words. We already know about hosting – so when we start to think about leading as being hosting, we instantly understand a lot, all of it rooted in our existing knowledge and experience. The wonderful thing about hosting is that there is so much to it. We find that exploring the details of hosting, the different ways to think about it, and different practices from around the world helps enormously to expand awareness and potential for new action. You are in just the right place, near the start of the book, to explore and expand your leadership, building on what you already know and do.

You use the word *host* – what about *hostess*?

Ah, yes, "The hostess with the mostest." Hosting has both masculine and feminine aspects to it. We find that women are equally good at hosting, and can take hosting ideas into leadership very smoothly. The metaphor seems to appeal in a different way than that of Servant-Leadership, valuable though that idea is. The word *hostess* has become rather devalued over the years – people used to talk about "air hostesses," as many in that role were women. There are also unfortunate connotations of the word, particularly in Asia, about women who hang out in bars. So, we don't like the word *hostess* very much. Throughout the book, when we talk about *host*, we are using the word in a gender-neutral way – it applies to women and men.

Can hosts have a purpose or intention – apart from looking after their guests?

One early reaction we had to the idea of Host Leadership was about how the relationship connects with a common task. Professor John Adair, well known for his task/team/individual model, wondered about how hosts and guests could come together for a common task. To us, this does not seem to be an issue, once we get to the idea that a host can invite people to join them in something, rather than simply look after them. There are many examples of this, from the student who invites his/her friends to help move stuff into a new flat with the promise of a good night's fun afterwards, to the more tacit expectations of the charity-ball organizers inviting wealthy people to their glittering event with celebrity auction. There is a great deal more to hosting than simply organizing some catering, as we will see.

I didn't invite my team! I inherited them when I took the job.

This is, of course, a very common situation. So in this case, using the Inviter role is probably not the best place to start. The Host Leadership metaphor is a rich and varied one, and you will find some other way to begin to work with your team. The point is to think like a host and see where that takes you – rather like Nelson Mandela introducing his "guard of honor" in prison in the opening chapter. You might like to do some listening to see what might be initiated, or look at the space you are creating, or do some connecting...

One thing to start with is to remember that hosting is about a relationship. So, get together with your team members, either one-on-one or in small groups, and spend some time finding out about them as people, as well as about what they do for the organization and what their concerns are. This could mean taking the chance to be "with the guests" (in the terminology of our four positions for a Host Leader – more details in the next chapter). Or you might even invite some of them into your "kitchen" for a focused and personal discussion. In a competitive job market, you may even end up wanting to invite them to stay.

My boss is not at all hostly! What can I do?

This is a question we get all the time. Two possibilities jump out. First, you can start thinking of yourself as a guest, and see how that produces ideas for working with your boss. What would a good guest do in your situation? Maybe it's bringing a little something useful or nice to the next meeting? Maybe you can help with the clearing up in some small way? Maybe you can ask about bringing some useful person with you to a forthcoming planning session? Maybe there's an opportunity to do some connecting with your boss? Maybe there is something that you could offer to initiate, and you could invite your boss to be involved in some specific way?

You can also start to think of yourself as a host to those around you – Host Leadership is not solely the privilege of the top dog. As we saw above, we can host at all levels of the organization. So, invite some people to discuss an important issue. Help to make your space more useful, recognizable and engaging. Make connections. And read on.

We will be presenting more detail on the four positions and six roles of a Host Leader in the following chapters. Remember, these are roles we can choose to step into (or out of), and positions we can take up. It is a very different task from trying to build "rules" that we have to follow all the time. You can use the roles and positions very flexibly, to produce an action which matches the situation and takes it forward in whatever direction you wish. Sometimes rapid progress will be possible; at other moments your best next step may be preparatory. Waiting for the right moment is a vital part of hosting and leadership.

Reflective questions

When you are facing a leadership challenge, we suggest you ask yourself these three questions:

- Do I want to step forward or back now?

- In which role do I want to step forward next?

- Which position(s) might I take up next?

You may already find some possibilities coming to you, from your previous experience. (Remember, we all know how to host already, at some level.) This book will help you remain alert to new possibilities, enrich your ideas and options, help you to find steps to nudge things along and show you how to act in a timely way to build engagement, performance and results.

Key points

➢ Hosts set context, give protection and enable community.

➢ Even in simple domestic settings, hosts carry out a myriad of tasks and roles.

➢ The key question for a host (and a Host Leader): *Should I step forward or step back?*

➢ In this book, we will look at six roles and four positions for a Host Leader.

➢ You don't need to be a formal "leader" to think and act like a host and thereby build connection and positive interaction.

4

A User's Guide to the Future

"The horizon leans forward, Offering you space to place new steps of change."

~Maya Angelou, On the Pulse of Morning

This chapter will center on our *User's Guide to the Future,* which illuminates the responsiveness of hosting and helps Host Leaders think about where to put their focus, how to connect long-term hopes and objectives with short-term action. Throughout the book we have been keeping this question at the front of our minds:

Am I going to step forward, or step back?

Stepping forward means taking action. Stepping back means being aware, noticing what is happening, preparing to step forward again at the right time. This outlook of rapidly alternating between acting and responding shows a basic truth: we don't fully know what's going to happen next. If we did, we wouldn't need to stay aware and alert to possibilities.

This chapter will look at how we can be in a complex and emerging world – a world where the future is uncertain and total knowledge is impossible. We will see how much management theory is based on the opposite understanding – that we can know and predict the future, and the one who can do it best will win.

In the financial world, projects are appraised using the system known as net present value. Remember the old saying, "A bird in the hand is worth two in the bush"? It's the same with money. Money you get today is worth its face value. Money you are scheduled to get next month is worth less than today's money, as there is a risk it won't arrive. Money arriving in a year's time is therefore worth even less, and so on. Accounting folk call this *discounted cash flow,* and there are frequent discussions in the financial world about exactly how much less cash will be worth in a year's time than it is right now.

Surprisingly, what most people don't seem to be aware of is that the same kind of reasoning applies to their plans... but with a twist. Our ideas about the future also become less reliable, less certain and less valuable as time goes on. Welcome to our *User's Guide to the Future*.

The User's Guide

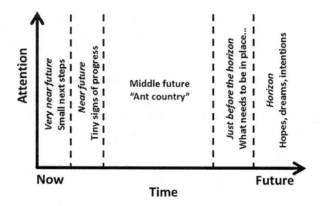

Time runs from left to right in this diagram. On the right, in the relatively distant future, are hopes, dreams and intentions – the *horizon*. These set the direction for everything else. Coming back in time towards the present are these elements:

- Hopes, dreams and intentions

- What needs to be in place to support the better future?

- "Ant country" (more on this in a moment)

- Tiny signs of progress

- Next steps right now

The actual timescales of these elements depend very much on the environment and industry in question. Mark's previous career in power stations meant looking forward several decades to see how the country's energy might be supplied. In Internet start-ups, even three months might be over the horizon.

As we will see in this chapter, to be a host is to accept uncertainty. When people come to your house, you never quite know what is going to happen. You can have hopes and intentions, how you'd like it to be, of course. But there is always the chance of something unexpected. This is built into our *User's Guide to the Future*. The guide outlines a way of working that is both efficient – getting lots of action for less effort – and responsive to the unfolding future. Let's see how it works.

Hopes, dreams and intentions

As Host Leaders, we will wish to accept and embrace the uncertainties of the future and stay flexible, while moving in the right direction. In that case, the key feature of the future is the horizon – our hopes, dreams and intentions. What do we really want to achieve here? What difference will that make – to us, to our organizations, to our families? Who else will benefit? How will the world (or even our work team or business) be a better place?

You can allocate these a time dimension – or not. We would advise not doing so in the first instance. Just take your time to think broadly about what you're seeking in the long run… Pause… That's it. Is this *really* worth pursuing? Do you want it enough to put in some actual energy right now? Maybe there is something related to this which would be more energizing for you?

Try and sum this up for yourself. Maybe make an elevator pitch – can you summarize it in thirty seconds? What is it about, who benefits, how do they benefit? Suppose it happened tomorrow; what might the world be like?

Hosting around the world: All together at the Sunday Assembly.

The starting of the Sunday Assembly – the so-called "atheist church" – is a good example of someone having a hope or dream and then acting on it. Sanderson Jones and Pippa Evans are both London-based stand-up comedians. During a long car journey to a gig, they discovered that they had a shared dream: both had been churchgoers in their youth, had stopped believing in God, and yet missed the community and stimulation of a regular gathering. How would it be if there was a "godless congregation," with singing, talks, readings, reflection, community, tea and cake?

As performers, the pair knew how to put on a show, so they decided to organize such an event, which they thought might draw a couple of dozen like-minded people. However, it turned out that others shared this dream: their initial "service" drew over 200 people, and within a year there were twenty-six congregations meeting around the world. Sunday Assembly hosts community for a group of people who have previously been ignored.

This hope or dream might be big or small. It might be global or very local indeed. It might be something relevant to everyone, or just to you. Whatever, something that sets a desired direction of travel is vital. Without that, any way might be the right way.

What has to be in place in the better future?

Looking nearly to the horizon, we can think back a little. Supposing we were to achieve the better future – what building blocks will have to be in place to support that? This is sometimes called *back-casting*, and it's about adding a bit more flesh to the bones of our hopes. This can help in large-scale projects, those involving many people, or those with long time scales.

Suppose we are looking to introduce a new product to the marketplace. What has to be in place? This will of course depend on the exact situation, but some typical key elements might include a tested product, identified target market, what benefits the product offers, marketing messages, packaging, distribution/ availability, pricing, and so on.

Note that we don't need the answers to these questions yet. These will emerge with time and work. However, simply knowing that these factors will (probably) be important helps us to frame the way in which the horizon connects with the now.

Hosting is about bringing people together in a common cause. Building ideas about the desired horizon can be a very good way to start to attract people, who can then be invited and engaged in building progress.

The role of a goal

A goal, it has been said, is a dream with a deadline. We have already seen the importance of hopes, dreams and aspirations in setting the direction to work in. What's the role of goals in all this?

Setting a goal may be a very sensible step in further defining the distant future. To launch a new product in time for next summer's market, for example, is a clearer statement than simply launching a new product. When we are in a position to set our own goals, this can work well.

The situation can be different in large organizations, where goals and targets can rain down from above. One way to work with this is to treat these targets as another part of the horizon. When we embrace dynamic steering, below, it will become clearer that it's impossible to say with complete confidence right now what will make sense in a month's time, let alone a year. What we *can* do, however, is to start to make some progress today.

Connecting with the horizon

Maya Angelou, in her poem *On the Pulse of Morning*, writes, "The horizon leans forward, Offering you space to place new steps of change." This is an important idea in the *User's Guide to the Future*. The horizon – the hopes, dreams, intentions and their precursors – is not distant years-away vague and fuzzy thoughts. We can help it to lean forward, to reach out to us, to mean something *today*. The way to do that is surprisingly simple – small next steps.

Small next steps

We have decided on a hope, dream or intention to work on… the next step may well be to look not at a plan to get all the way there, but at some next steps right now. This makes particular sense in the world of wicked problems, as each step will change the situation in ways which are hard to foresee.

Facing a situation where large changes are required, it is tempting to jump to a particular conclusion: big movements require big plans. What could be more impressive than a massive budget, a detailed action plan, multiple Gantt charts … And then what?

It's great to think big. But turning thought into action, the benefits of "big" are less clear. We have all seen grand plans turn to naught, in the face of the inevitable collision with the real world – the real world where things go wrong, people's interest shifts, accidents happen, fashions change and the unexpected lurks around every corner.

Here is a counterintuitive thought: the bigger the thing you want to achieve, the smaller the first step. Sounds crazy? Let's think about it. Benefits to taking a smaller step rather than a big one include:

• Can be done more quickly (like today or tomorrow)

• Can be done more confidently (it feels more within our control to do)

• Can be done without (or with less) permission from others

• Is more likely to get done, as it's only a small step

• Is therefore more likely to actually make an impact on the world (a small step taken makes far more impact than a big step *not* taken)…

• And therefore is more likely to produce some reaction – feedback, encouragement, data, impact, connection, whatever – that allows us to respond and plan another next step, to build on the results

• And … if the small step doesn't produce useful results, then you haven't wasted much time and energy and can go back for another think. After all, it was only a small step…

Hosts tend to deal in small steps. Small steps can give rapid feedback, as well as engaging others. Actually trying things out is very different than sitting and planning for months in an attempt to plot everything out before we start. In our experience, everything comes down to small steps. Some of these steps may be more significant than others, for sure. Some may in hindsight turn out to be crucial in unexpected ways. Even the biggest project – power-plant construction, social change, the digital revolution – comes down to small steps in the end.

In the Sunday Assembly, Sanderson and Pippa opted to put on an initial "godless congregation" service to see how it would go. As professional entertainers, they knew how to put on a show, where to find musicians, how to get a simple logo designed, how to get a bit of local press coverage… in their terms, these are all small steps. The response was not what they expected… but the power of this approach is to combine purposeful action with flexible responsiveness.

Moving in from each end of our *User's Guide to the Future*, there are other places we can go next, should we need to.

Tiny signs of progress

Another helpful adjunct is to think a little way into the future. What might be the first tiny signs of progress? Things that will let us know we're on the right track? Signs that things are progressing in a useful way? Signs are an interesting way to think about this – they are things we'd notice, not things we would do (those would be *next* steps... and remember that in dynamic steering we're going to decide the next steps when we get there, and concentrate for today on today's steps).

Having a good idea of the first signs of progress can be particularly useful in cases where the next steps are not obvious or seem tough or uncertain – rapid feedback will be useful in letting us know that what we're doing is working in some way, and moving us in roughly the right direction.

One small but illuminating example of this comes from Mark's exploits as an archaeologist during his student vacations. As a rookie, he was asked to dig out all the soil from a certain patch down to the bed rock. "Yes, sir!" said Mark, eager to please, and he started digging enthusiastically. After a short while, the soil became more yellow and crumbly, but no sign of the bed rock. On and on he dug, the heap of yellow earth getting bigger and bigger. After a couple of hours, the supervisor returned. "Aha!" said the supervisor. "Do you know what the bed rock looks like here?" "No," said Mark. "I assume it looks like rock..." It didn't look like rock at all – it was yellow and crumbly. The very stuff Mark had been shoveling in the hot sun for two hours. Because Mark didn't know how to read the signs of progress – in this case that he was at the bed rock – he didn't know how to respond next – and stop digging. An exhausting lesson in the power of tiny signs.

The missing middle – "Ant Country"

This area – somewhere in the middle distance, in between the signs of progress and the precursors to our hopes – is an area beloved of accountants and micro-managers. "Where will we be in a year's time? How much will the spend be in the third quarter? What food will I be eating on 28 March next year?" The first two questions are oft posed. The third is (we hope) patently ludicrous.

The concept of "ant country" was devised by British scientists and authors Jack Cohen and Ian Stewart[1] to reflect the immense richness, possibility and uncertainty of a complex and emerging future. Briefly, ant colonies (and mathematical models of ant colonies) are fine examples of *complex systems* – where interacting agents (in this case ants) respond and react to developing circumstances and each other to produce rich, useful yet unpredictable behavior. This is not to say that we are like ants – far from it – but the mathematical analogy holds.

One way that humans deal with this is to say that "stuff happens," shrug and get on with their lives. However, we are becoming more and more aware of the limits of predictability in life. Hopes for modeling using computers which were held up in the 1960s have fallen down in the face of the complexity of math, such that ever more complex and powerful computers make less and less progress in predicting even the weather, let alone the accidents and vicissitudes of life.

This is not to say that it's not worth looking at possible occurrences – good or bad – in the future. You *ARE* allowed to plan for crises and practice them! Mark used to work as a physicist at a nuclear power plant, where the management quite rightly spent time on emergency planning and practicing what would happen in an accident. The point about this is that it's not idly gazing into the middle distance; it's practicing something that *might* happen tomorrow – unlikely and undesirable, but it *might* happen and it's important to be prepared. That's not the same as practicing today for something that might happen in a year's time.

There is a clear message in the *User's Guide to the Future*: Don't worry overmuch about the middle part. In the end, it will come to be now (or a short time hence) and therefore get more important. This is not to say that we shouldn't plan, and of course stakeholders sometimes want some sort of confidence that we know what we're up to – but the details of what will happen in months or years may be best left as broad-brush ideas rather than being planned for in the same way as we look at next week.

Embrace dynamic steering

As a Host Leader, we will be getting skilled at holding two different elements in mind: a future intention, hope or goal; and great flexibility over exactly what steps may be required to make progress. Welcome to dynamic steering.

This is a philosophy running through modern rapid iteration methods such as agile project management, Holacracy® and Solutions Focus. Imagine riding a bike over a journey of a mile in the country, to the nearest store. You know where you want to get to – the store. Presumably you also know why you are going there – let's say to buy some supper to feed your family. So, you set out.

Now, the thing about riding a bike is that you're never absolutely in control of it. As you ride along, you maintain a course by adjusting the handlebars and shifting balance and weight distribution. At slow speeds, the way you move your knees turns out to be very important. Then there are bumps in the road, potholes, squirrels to avoid, cars and pedestrians, and so on. All of these require small adjustments to your steering.

Imagine we are at the beginning of the journey. I ask you exactly where you will be steering after 132 yards. If you think you know, then you haven't really learned how to ride a bike. You can't possibly know exactly what will be happening at that moment, and therefore where you will be needing to steer.[2]

Host Leaders know the power of dynamic steering. It's just the same as hosting a party – you can know you want to serve the food at eight p.m., but exactly what you'll be doing at eight p.m. on the dot, who knows? Hugging an old friend, introducing two strangers, listening to tales about your old friend Alex's new job, frantically scraping the burned bits off a roast chicken …

While having the intention to serve dinner at eight p.m. is fine and very useful, hosts use flexibility to allow their efforts to flow, match and fit in with the wider context of the event. And, who knows, you may even be able to serve dinner at eight p.m. on the dot… which means you had a little bit of luck, as well as some good skill.

Some of you may have noticed that this is an iterative way of doing things – keeping on moving in small steps, checking to see if the movement is in the right direction, and then moving again. What is different here is the potential timescale of the responses. When Mark started out on his career in the utility industry, things moved very slowly, and even an annual planning process seemed rather fast ("Is it that time of year again?"). In Agile project management, the iterations may be in terms of two-week sprints, perhaps with a daily check-in. In Holacracy®, decisions are deliberately left to the last responsible moment, to help ensure that the information on which they are based is as relevant as possible. Note that the "last responsible moment" is not the same as the *last* moment!

Host Leaders will probably want to work on this kind of timescale – and also on much faster reactions. At certain key points ("pinch points," which we will describe in the Co-Participator chapter later in the book), you may have to react in a matter of seconds.

Awareness

In order to act responsively, we need first to be **aware**. It's very hard to respond coherently without knowing what's happening around us. This awareness is something that Host Leaders develop over time. Most people find it easier to become aware of what's happening around them when they are not in the spotlight, but rather with the guests, as part of the group. This happens when we step back and join in. As we have seen in this book so far, this is not a move of abdication, but rather a change of pace which allows us access to different kinds of input. Being "one of the crowd" allows us to hear different voices and see things from different angles.

Have you ever been thinking of buying, say, a new car, and you ponder the options and get interested in a particular model of Volkswagen – and then you start to notice that particular model driving past, or parked near your home, or mentioned in the press? This is not magical (at least in an inexplicable way, although it is rather amazing). It's a natural part of the way humans act in the world, and psychologists call it *the frequency illusion*. If we are expecting to see something, or even if we've just been thinking about something, we are more alert to noticing it.

This is where the tiny signs of progress really come into their own. Having prepared ourselves, we will be more easily able to spot some of the signs that indicate movement in a useful direction. We can then be encouraged and reassured that things are developing.

Everything is a useful gift

It's tempting to view anything that happens and knocks things in an unexpected direction as "bad" or "unhelpful." From a predict-and-control mindset, of course, it is – the universe is showing us who is boss yet again. However, from a dynamic steering viewpoint, this is all part of the emergent process.

One good way to help us think about the possibilities of unexpected events – as opposed to the nuisance and disturbance – is to use the maxim "Everything is a useful gift."

Rather than cursing and immediately acting to throw the unexpected aside, we ask ourselves how the developments might be useful in some way to move towards our future hopes and intentions. This is not to say that absolutely everything IS a useful gift, of course ... However, thinking this way helps us to stop and consider the possibility.

Losing money produces a useful gift

Mark remembers an occasion when (for the only time so far in his career) a company owing him money for running a masterclass went into administration. The amount of money was modest, but still significant. What a nuisance! However, the same company also owed others far more – including some partners with whom he had worked on the project in question. The subsequent discussions about what to do about the impact (which had resulted in the partners nearly going out of business) led to closer relations and conversations about future projects... which led to Helen joining this project! A useful gift indeed. What seemed like a bad thing led to a much better thing.

In some circles, the idea of using what's there is called *utilization*. It's a key part of Mark's work in Solutions Focus too – the idea of working with what's in front of us (however unpromising that might look) rather than moaning about what isn't there (and therefore not making any actual progress at all). Mark's favorite example features jazz piano soloist legend Art Tatum – who was said to be able to play on the out-of-tune pianos he was forced to use on the road in the 1930s in such a way that the "bad" notes made musical sense, so the whole thing sounded great.[3]

Dreamer, Realist, Business Planner, Host

We have noticed over the years that different kinds of people treat and use the future differently. Let us look for a moment at three tempting but not altogether useful alternatives that you may, like us, recognize from your experience of life at work.

The Dreamer

The Dreamer is the person who sees a wonderful future ahead – a marvelous opportunity where things will be better, the world will be transformed; the possibilities are enormous and endless. They can often see this very clearly in their mind's eye. They give all their attention to expanding (and expounding) on the immense benefits and innate attraction of the better future.

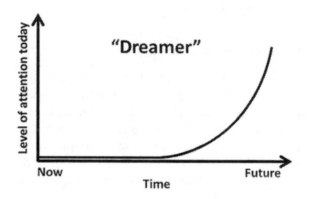

That's great, of course. However, the Dreamer seems unwilling or unable to put actual steps in place that can build towards this future. Perhaps the whole task seems so big that any actual step is petty by comparison, not worthy of the goal. Perhaps such a big future should seem to be matched by a big plan of action – which never actually gets off the ground. It may even be the case that the Dreamer is a bit incompetent and can't organize him/herself. (In which case, of course, they need a friend who can …) The dream remains just that – and meanwhile, the Dreamer continues to fixate on it, expand on it, and probably gets frustrated that nothing is happening and nobody shares the dream.

The Realist

The Realist is rather the opposite of the Dreamer. The Realist is very keen to make sure that things happen, and will go out of his/her way to chase actions, make plans, be organized and get stuff done. They will know what needs doing, who is doing what, what is happening next. Wonderfully useful people to have in your organization.

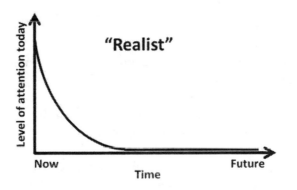

However, the Realist doesn't let themselves be bothered by where things are going in the long term. Doing today's work as well as possible is the thing. They might think that long-term hopes and dreams are a recipe for disappointment. They might be suspicious, having been faced with reorganization after reorganization, that any long-term goal will inevitably be thwarted by "them" (on the Board, in the market, in power). They may (with some justification) agree with Doris Day that "*Que sera sera, Whatever will be will be.*" The future is not ours to see, of course. However, our thoughts today about possible futures can certainly influence what we do.

The Business Planner

The Business Planner orientation is not as prevalent as it once was. However, we still notice it appearing in some places and want to point it out, so that you can be wary. Business plans are (or used to be) concerned with things on a middle-future timescale – one to three years, perhaps. What is the cash flow for the first year? How much profit may appear in year two? And given all that, how much might the business be worth at the end of year three?

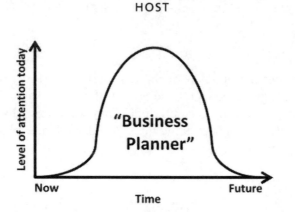

The phrase "given all that" is the big giveaway here. By looking at a middle timescale, the plan can take our eyes off the most important areas. Yes, of course there needs to be some attention given to whether the organization could possibly survive. However, as we will see in a moment, in a moving, complex and uncertain world, the classical business plan is only as good as its assumptions. These exercises can easily turn into mere arithmetic ("assuming growth of twenty percent per year…") and rapidly become detached from reality. The Business Planner spends much of their time in "ant country."

Now let us look at a more useful orientation to the future.

The Host

Hosts are always open to changes and uncertainty. This is why we focus all the time on stepping forward and back, on maneuverability and flexibility. However, hosts also have a focus on their long-term hopes, dreams and aspirations – the direction in which they seek to move. And they don't get bogged down in "ant country." So, the Host will use the future in this fashion:

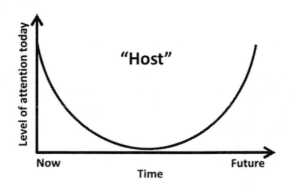

Focusing on the near future – practical next steps and signs of progress – and the distant future – hopes, intentions and their precursors – is the trademark of a good Host.

Reflective questions

• What kind of timescale makes sense for your particular *User's Guide to the Future*? Months? Years? Weeks?

• How clear are you about your horizon – your hopes, dreams and intentions?

• How are you bringing them forward – to live in your life today?

• What helps you connect with the idea of dynamic steering?

• How can you let go more of wanting to plan the whole way? How can you avoid getting bogged down in "ant country?"

• How clear are you about your tiny next steps?

Key points

➢ The *User's Guide to the Future* shows that not every element of the future is seeable or useable in the same way.

➢ The horizon, although it may be in the far distance, is vital in terms of setting a direction for progress.

➢ Bring the horizon into the present with tiny next steps.

➢ The middle distance – "ant country" – is potentially a burden. It's too far away to know effectively and can be a distraction.

➢ Embrace dynamic steering to avoid getting trapped in worrying about "ant country" – take action, make adjustments, keep learning.

5

Four Positions for a Host Leader

"Both in and out of the game, and watching and wondering at it."

~Walt Whitman, Song of Myself

One of the challenges of being a host is that our attention is divided. If you're anything like us, you will be familiar with the classic hosting challenge – when a meal is being cooked, and the guests are waiting in another room, how can we be in two places at once? There are all kinds of ways to deal with this in the hosting situation. Maybe one host entertains the guests while another works in the kitchen? The modern trend for kitchen-dining rooms also alleviates this particular difficulty.

In Host Leadership, we have to split our attention and time in even more ways. During the research for this book, we have spoken with many hosts and many leaders. It is clear that there are at least four key positions for a Host Leader. Let's remind ourselves of the four positions.

In the spotlight – Being the focus of attention, out front, making things happen

With the guests – Still out front, but being "one of the group" – not the center of attention

 **In the gallery** – Standing back, taking an overview of what's happening

In the kitchen – In a more private and intimate space, preparing and reflecting

We will now take a more in-depth look at each position.

In the spotlight

 Being in the spotlight is very much the public-facing part of the leader's role. It is where the action is, in full view of everyone – and everything about you gives off messages.

Leadership writer Simon Walker describes this as "The version of ourselves we show the world." Being successful in the spotlight is about standing up with confidence, owning the space and having presence. Good front-stage leaders are real and authentic, which builds trust and confidence in the people around them.

We find that many leaders are naturally comfortable with this, and indeed see it as the main aspect of their work. There are ways to become more at ease on a stage, or when giving a presentation. Some find it nerve-wracking and uncomfortable – it is well known that speaking in public is regarded by many as only slightly less stress-inducing than death.

The sorts of occasion when we are in the spotlight might include:

*   Representing your organization, headquarters or team – during factory visits, branch inspections, peer review gatherings, stakeholder consultation groups

*   Making presentations – inside and outside the organization, formal and informal

- Facilitating workshops and discussion groups. Good facilitators have a very good sense of when to step forward, even though they aim to spend most of the time allowing people to get on with the work – inside and outside the organization, formal and informal.

Time in the spotlight is time when we have our leader's hat firmly in place. On these occasions, we are definitely being observed by all present as the leader, as the person who is seen to be at the top – even if we are being facilitative and participative in our style.

Stepping forward into attention and focus

Being in the spotlight is very much a stepping-forward position. You are asking for attention, to be heard. What many people who shun the limelight don't realize is that there are definite skills to being able to command attention. What is more, these begin *before* stepping forward.

There are whole books on how to present an attitude of confidence in front of an audience. This does not entail turning into an actor or stand-up comedian, or carrying out a whole series of meditation and relaxation exercises (though if you find those help, then by all means go ahead). A few of our favorite tips include:

Prepare well ... and then let go: There are two ways to look unconfident in front of a group. One is to be ill-prepared and flounder. The second, less obvious, is to be very well prepared and then to stick rigidly to the plan. This looks forced and very unrelaxed; the muscles tighten, the audience knows that they are mere onlookers with no input or relevance, and everyone rapidly starts to wonder when the ordeal will be over.

By all means, prepare yourself for what you want to say. The trick is then to let go and trust that your preparation will do its work. You know what you want to say (in principle); you may even have a comforting list of key points in your hand. Run through them before you step into the spotlight, and then... start! On its own, this might sound a bit scary, so you can then use the next tip......

Warm up – even a little: Anyone wishing to put themselves forward at their best will warm up first. Top performers in both the sports and arts worlds would not dream of stepping onto the stage without a full warming-up process – because it makes such a difference to their impact. The greatest impact is often at the start of the performance, which is also the most important time when it comes to capturing your audience's attention. If the start is electrifying and engaging, people will look up and give great attention – which reinforces the confidence of the performer. It's a virtuous circle.

When we step into the spotlight as leaders, the same thing applies. We are not suggesting a full routine of stretching, singing scales, gargling with whisky or running on the spot (unless you really want to, of course – and then find a spot out of sight!). Take a few deep breaths. Move your shoulders around to feel your upper body. Focus and appreciate the feel of your feet on the floor. Shake your hands briefly and vigorously to get a tingle into your fingers. Try it – particularly if you are nervous about asking for everyone's attention.

Know your opening line: While it's excellent practice to know what to say and then let go, one great tip is to know, in detail, how you intend to start. What's the first thing you want to say, to capture your audience's attention and to set the tone for your time in the spotlight? Just the first line – the rest will come as you proceed. Two things don't work terribly well as openers. One is a fumbled or confused line. The other is an apology. So if things are running late, or there have been difficulties getting people together, don't *start* with the apology. Give a warm welcome and get things underway – then offer a brief apology and move on.

Know when it's time to step back again: It's a good idea to know what we are hoping will happen when our time in the spotlight is up. What will happen next? Who is next up to speak? What are we hoping to lead into? What response do we want? One skill of being in the spotlight is to pass it on well, so the next person has a good start and everyone who is watching knows what is happening and where they should be looking.

Stepping back is a very positive move, particularly from a Host Leadership perspective. We step back to allow and encourage others to step forward. This move is not an end, but a new beginning. In the old days of totalitarian leaders, giving a five-hour speech was seen as a move of great authority. We wonder whether they simply didn't know how to step back.

With the guests

A Host Leader knows the value of spending time with his/her guests. This is also time spent in public, although the focus will be different. Rather than being in the spotlight, with all eyes on him/her, the leader can take time to go around and "work the room." This is a much less formal process, and often involves spending time with people individually or in very small groups. This is not a time of formal business. It's time for catching up, asking how the person is getting on, connecting with others. This is time for discovering and remembering people's strengths, interests, particular concerns, and so on.

Who are the "guests?"

We have already seen how the concept of guest is intimately linked with the concept of host – they are mutually co-defining. So, just as *host* is a metaphor for leading, then *guest* is also a metaphor – for the others, those who are around, who are following, participating, co-working, cooperating. A key part of leading as a host is to start thinking of the others as guests, and seeing what difference that makes to relationships and (often instinctive) actions and responses. We may or may not have actually invited them along (and there will be much more about this in the Inviter chapter later in the book), but here they are. So, "guests" might be staff, suppliers, colleagues, associates, customers, students, delegates, etc.

Chances to be with the guests include:

- Attend a meeting that you're not leading

- Let other people lead on certain agenda items and you can join in the discussion along with the other guests (attendees)

- Attend an event that's taking place – perhaps an open day or a supplier/customer visit

- Go along with others on a sales meeting or an installation, a customer going "live"

- Eat lunch in the staff room

- Mingle over a coffee break

Why do these things? Because we find out so much more! We hear about things from the experience and perspective of others. It's a real listening position, which feeds into the Initiator role – we can identify opportunities and learn what's really happening, what's getting in the way, what would improve things.

Which guests are we spending time with?

John Oliver was CEO of Leyland Trucks in the UK. At the time, the latest management theory was advocating "managing by wandering around," so John had his diary card to remind him to take a walk down to the factory floor every day. Every day, he would go down and talk to the same people – the people who talked to him. Then one day, a guy handed in his resignation, and when asked why, he said that people weren't listened to or asked their opinion. Of course, this came as a surprise, since John went down to talk to people every day. The reply was that he only ever talked to the negative people – in fact they became known as the BMWs – bitchers, moaners, whingers.[1]

While it is easy and tempting to focus on those making a noise and asking for attention, a great Host Leader will make sure to spend time with as many people as possible, and in particular to seek out those who may be on the fringes rather than those loudly declaiming in the middle.

It is also important to remember that the objective of spending time in this manner is to *be with* people, rather than to *avoid* them. Mark remembers meeting a power-plant manager who proudly told him that he was out in the factory every morning and so really knew what was going on. On being asked about what exact time he carried out this interaction, the manager was even more proud. "Seven a.m., at the end of the night shift! That way there's hardly anyone around, and I can get it done very quickly – fantastic for time management..." Hmm. What is the priority here – really being with people, or getting back to the office as quickly as possible?

Get out and get under!

There was a popular song in the early days of motoring: *He'd Have To Get Under* by Billy Murray. Released on wax cylinders and early phonograph records in 1913, the song relates how the hero's efforts to woo his sweetheart in his jalopy are constantly thwarted by mechanical misfortune. The car breaks down again and again, so in the chorus he has to "get out and get under" to fix it. It's a fun song – look it up on YouTube.

For a Host Leader, "get out and get under" is not an unfortunate occurrence; it's an excellent maxim. By getting out – being with people in one-to-one or small-group settings – we can really get under what they are thinking and saying, connect with them and build relationship and trust.

Some leaders find that it's a challenge to get enough time with people in the position of "being with the guests." Yes, it can be challenging – particularly if you don't do it! The trick is to find times when you can be with people – managing by walking about, going to events as "one of the group" rather than as The Leader, making it our business to *make* time for a little informal contact.

Mark remembers a chief executive from his early career who spent as little time as he could outside his defended office emplacement (surrounded by doors and secretaries) because he was nervous and worried he wouldn't find anything to say. So he never went outside. Consequently, people didn't really know who he was, and contact was gradually lost. This is, of course, a self-fulfilling prophecy: if he had even spent a *little* time out and about, he would have been a more familiar face and people might have been able to put him at his ease a little more, contact could have been built up, and so on.

These first two positions – in the spotlight and with the guests – can be considered to be stepped-forward positions. We are with other people, focused on them, interacting with them, and listening to them. The other two positions – in the gallery and in the kitchen – are more stepped back. They offer a chance to take in a bigger picture, reflect on what's going well and what is needed next, and to learn and refresh ourselves.

In the gallery

We have already introduced the idea that the gallery is another position where leaders might spend time. Harvard University leadership guru Ronald A. Heifetz has written extensively about "leadership from the balcony" as an essential practice for effective leadership.[2] It is about leaders intentionally shifting their perspective in fundamental ways to look creatively at the whole team, the organization and the whole community in which you work.

The gallery, as we propose it, is a place high above the action. From there, the room can be surveyed from a position above the hubbub and interaction down where the party is happening. In castles and grand houses, there was often such a gallery, mainly used by musicians. Often it was somewhat hidden and not in full view of the people gathered below. From a spot such as this, it's possible to take an overview, to see what's happening without (for a few moments) the distraction of being downstairs. Different patterns are visible; the different ways in which people are participating (or not) become clearer.

Whilst this gallery is, of course, another metaphor, sometimes it can be a real as well as a metaphorical position. Legendary London restaurateur Anton Mosimann has a small table in the top corner in the balcony of his dining club – an excellent spot from which to quietly keep an eye on events in the restaurant below. We are not proposing that you install a platform in your office! (Though that might be an interesting strategy…) Time in the gallery is time observing from a different position. In our normal work life, this might include:

•   Stepping back from everyday business and distraction

•   Taking a pause to look at the big picture

•   Taking a "helicopter view" – looking from above at wider issues, progress and challenges ahead

A Host Leader will take time in the gallery to overview the situation and revise his/her plans accordingly. One challenge is to not only spend time in gallery positions in our organizations, but to shift our perspectives to allow us to see things differently; for example, "If I were a customer here, how would it be? What would I notice? What would I want?"

Don't just do something – stand there

Although this idea of a gallery is, of course, metaphorical, the actual practice of simply standing somewhere different is a surprisingly good way to gain new and valuable input on how your organization is functioning. We have all heard the action-oriented cry, "Don't just stand there – do something!" Well, being in the gallery is a fine chance to take the *opposite* position. Time in the gallery is not for leaping to conclusions and shouting orders for change (except perhaps in the direst emergency). It is much more about taking in the view, enjoying a change of perspective from the normal hurly-burly and quietly noticing what is happening. What is noticed can then be put into practice in one of the other positions – an attention-grabbing spotlight moment (high impact), a few quiet words with some of the guests, or perhaps a topic for discussion with some key advisors in the kitchen.

Earlier in her career, Helen was a service quality manager with a UK bank. She regularly visited branch offices and chose different places to sit or stand to view what was happening in the branch. This was time she spent "in the gallery," from where she was able to gain a new perspective on the customers' experience of the branch. How are the team members interacting? How do they and the branch appear to customers? What is the flow of customers like? Where are the bottlenecks? How do customers use the facilities? As a visitor to the gallery, she could see things that the branch manager had stopped seeing. With this in mind, Helen often took the branch manager with her into the gallery to share a new view of the branch.

Helen also led workshops to help staff improve their customer service. She found gallery work to be essential throughout any session. Being on the gallery enabled her to take a step back, to gain a perspective on how the group was working together. She could ask herself questions such as, "What am I learning about this group and about each individual? What is working? What might I change or do differently?" These gallery questions may be specifically about the content of the session or they may be wider; for example, what are we learning about the culture of the organization? How do people work together? What rituals exist around here? How do things operate in the organization?

Being ready to jump in

Another advantage of having a position in the gallery is that, if emergencies arise, we are in a great position to survey what is going on, make some quick decisions and then step forward to intervene. We may want to step forward quietly and sort out something that may cause a problem, or have a quiet word with someone to make sure they are aware of what's going on. Sometimes we may even have to step forward into the spotlight, to take control and let everyone know what is happening and what do to next. This is one of the moments where the tips on stepping forward, in the section above, can really come into play.

In the chapter on the role of Co-Participator, we will be discussing the idea of pinch points – the times when something crucial is happening and the Host Leader will want to be there, even if they are not leading the proceedings from the spotlight. The gallery position offers a great place at these times – if everything goes well, one can be there to applaud and appreciate; and the chance to step in if absolutely necessary is always open as well.

Seeing the wood – *and* the trees

Spending time in the gallery stops us from "being so absorbed in the game that we get carried away with it." It enables us to "see the forest *as well as* the trees." And it helps us, in the words of Walt Whitman in his poem, *Song of Myself,* to be "*Both in and out of the game, and watching and wondering at it.*"

Why is this important? We are all familiar with how the detail can distract from the bigger picture. Detail is vital for a Host Leader – and so is the big picture. That's why we spend time both with the guests (seeing and hearing about the details from different perspectives) and also take time in the gallery, to see the patterns, connections and emerging order from a new perspective.

Getting the gallery view from others

What if you are temporarily stuck in the spotlight, and want a view from the gallery? Take a lesson from NASCAR and have someone else do it for you. In the USA, motor sport is typically run on high-speed oval tracks with cars running inches apart at over 200 mph, and the slightest mistake can mean disaster. The development of radio in the 1970s meant that a direct audio channel to the driver was possible, and during the subsequent decade many teams began to use "spotters." These people were usually in positions atop the grandstands with the remit to pass information directly to the driver; this might be general news about the track and other racers, or very specific calls on the moment to pull back onto the racing line after passing a competitor. This worked so well in terms of increasing safety that in the late 1980s, NASCAR mandated that every driver must have a spotter.

In a work environment, this might mean having a trusted colleague moving around, taking in what is going on and letting you know from time to time. Yasuteru Aoki organizes great Solutions Focus conferences in Japan from time to time, and is helped by his wife Ruiko. She pops up all over the place – usually with a camera in her hand. In the program, she is listed as the photographer, but she is actually playing an even more important role: feeling how things are going and passing on a wider view of proceedings. And she also takes great photos as a record of the event.

In the kitchen

The other place where Host Leaders spend time is "in the kitchen." The kitchen is the most private place for the host – although others may come in, this is usually by invitation only. This position was inspired by the "back-stage" metaphor of Simon Walker in his trilogy Undefended Leadership.[3] This is where we plan, prepare, reflect, work on our own development, seek counsel from confidants, etc.

As a host, we will invariably sometimes retreat to the kitchen. This is a more private place – where preparation is done, where family members may come and go, but which the guests are normally steered away from. A classic hosting dilemma is whether to be with our guests – engaging and interacting – or whether to be in the kitchen preparing food – which naturally is also very important.

As we've already acknowledged, many people nowadays have kitchen-dining rooms, and in our everyday lives this distinction has become less important. For the purposes of our Host Leadership metaphor, however, the kitchen will be the place in which we work in private, out of view of most of the guests.

Hosting around the world: The people behind the curtain

In ancient times in Japan, a samurai (warrior)'s glory was possible often due to their wife's substantial yet hidden support at home. Wives never took credit for it. But the greater the sacrifice, the more people knew about it and paid respect. It was referred to as *naijo-no kou* (the effect of hidden help). In modern times, Japan is also home to many accomplished businesspeople who are known to have partners who support their husbands effectively in many unseen ways. The partners take pride in putting their secret effort behind the curtain because of this tradition of honoring *naijo-no-kou*.

In Japan and elsewhere it is still common to host in teams. It is very important to credit everyone involved, particularly those who cannot be seen and whose contribution may therefore be harder for the guests to notice and appreciate. Who in your organization would you honor with naijo-no-kou? If you haven't noticed anyone yet, look for them!

Reflective practice in the kitchen

We have already acknowledged the importance of working behind the scenes. Highly effective people know the value of time spent in the kitchen – they recognize the need to continually develop themselves. Stephen Covey, author of *The 7 Habits of Highly Effective People*, called it "sharpening the saw."[4]

It is widely recognized that reflective practice is a vital discipline for leaders. But what is reflective practice? It is analyzing experiences to learn from them – and cultivating habits of reflective practice ensures we continuously learn and grow. Reflective practice or "work in the kitchen" can include time to think and plan. This includes both reflecting and learning from past experiences, and preparing for the next ones. It includes having a support network, maybe a coach or mentor, participating in a peer group activity to learn from others in a similar situation to yours. If we are going to present the best version of ourselves to the world, we do it by balancing the public work – in the spotlight, with the guests and even in the gallery – with more private work.

Swedish consultant Malin Morén runs the successful Lorensbergs firm in Gothenburg. With offices in China and South Africa as well as in Europe, there is always plenty going on. Malin has found an excellent way to get her time in the kitchen, which also fits in with her lifestyle. Most every evening, she and her husband/chief executive Trevor Durnford go for a long walk with their dogs! They spend an hour talking about which customers are doing what, the latest feedback from their staff, new possibilities, dangers to watch out for – and also get some great exercise and company.

Making time for the kitchen

One thing we find again and again in our work supporting leaders around the world is that most of them say that they could use more time in the kitchen. The challenge is – when to do it? If we pack our diary full of public activities, where is the space for work in the kitchen? We know quite a few leaders who use traveling time – in the car, on the train – to reflect on their work, but that's not usually a chance to engage with others about it, or give it the quality of attention it deserves.

Helen recalls her time as a service quality manager when she was quite typical in this thinking. Yes, she used her travelling time as well as possible, but how much of that time was she running on empty? And then when she got home, she was probably straight into time with the family. What about nourishment? Recharging? Never mind some kitchen work where she considered what she'd learned that day and what she might do differently as a result. What about taking a step back, replaying the day to get a different perspective? What about planning for her next front-stage performance? Kitchen time helps us stay connected with the bigger picture. What are we here to deliver? What else is going on that we might need to know about or that might affect us? It was such a valuable lesson that she now ensures she regularly builds her time "in the kitchen" into her week.

Finding time for regenerating in the kitchen

We met Derek a couple of years ago. Derek is the owner and managing director of Mobysoft. Founded in 2003, Mobysoft has developed into one of the UK's leading suppliers of intelligent data solutions to social housing. With over fifty social housing clients across the UK, Mobysoft has a well-founded reputation for delivering highly innovative solutions that consistently deliver return on investment in this sector.

Derek is really good at his "in the kitchen" work. He's not afraid to ask for help. He has a team around him who can help with the learning and change that's required of him as the business grows. He is an exception in recognizing that a growing business demands him to learn and change. The team includes a non-exec director, a coach and a mentor, each of whom he has selected for their different skills and experiences.

Derek doesn't want these people to tell him what to do; rather, he values their insight, their questions and the challenge they bring to him. These people all act as sounding boards for him – after all, being a managing director can be a lonely place. Taking time out of the business to spend with these people means he takes time to reflect, think and plan. These meetings often ensure he focuses on strategy rather than staying caught up in the day-to-day demands of running a business.

Derek has learned the benefit of building reflection time into his week. On a Friday morning, he goes early to his favorite table in a restaurant, orders his usual Friday breakfast and spends time alone reflecting on the week: reviewing his notes of key points from the week (which he's noted in a notebook during the week), and then taking another step back to consider what he's learned from the week that he can take into his planning for the following week. He found creating a structure or process around his reflection really worked for him. It suited his natural style.

When Derek is regularly doing his kitchen work, his "in the spotlight" public presence is stronger. When we are in the spotlight, we are in the full view of everyone, and everything about us gives off messages. Kitchen time keeps us congruent and authentic. It maintains the trust and confidence of those around us. It is all a balance, and when we are out of balance it shows. When Derek is out of balance, his team can tell. What is great is that he knows and does something about it.

Different ways to use your kitchen

Derek's example shows some of the ways in which a senior manager might make sure they take some time in the kitchen on a regular basis. Other possible ways to get private reflection and learning opportunities include:

- Making time with a coach or mentor for regular conversations

- Keeping a regular learning journal

- Organizing team awaydays or focused retreats

- Joining a mastermind group, action learning set, supervision team or other similar place for discussion with experienced folk from outside your organization

- Using mindfulness methods to take a brief respite from the busyness of the day

Most people find they need to work hard initially to build these things into their routines. However, it's really worthwhile doing it. So, get your organizer, diary or phone out – and when you find something that works for you, make it into a regular event.

Using all four positions – a sparkling start with an open day

Helen was working with a company providing bespoke manufacturing installations solutions around the world from their base in the north of England. The company had decided to offer an open day at their premises, to showcase products and services in their fabulous new offices and show room. It fell to shop manager Joanne to get the day organized and running, with ten existing and potential customers signed up to attend.

Joanne had involved all her team in the preparation for the event, with each of them leading on a particular part of the day. There were to be practical demonstrations, information sessions, viewing of products and product training. None of the team had been involved in such a day before and all had put in a lot of hard work and preparation. Nevertheless as the day approached, nerves were running high. Then, two days before the event the team found out the day was to be filmed. This cranked up the pressure still further. As emotions approached fever pitch, the team were all doubting their ability to deliver.

Joanne was acutely aware how people were feeling and wondered how best she could support them. She too was feeling the pressure – she felt the weight of the day on her shoulders and wanted it to go well for all the team. She wasn't sure how to use her time on the day – lead in the shop (her usual role), be prepared to cover for unexpected absences and crises, or what.

Helen introduced Joanne to Host Leadership and in particular the four positions a Host Leader might adopt:

- In the spotlight – there would be times when Joanne would need to spend time in the spotlight: out front, center stage, perhaps leading key sessions.

- With the guests – at key times during the day Joanne would have an opportunity to spend time with the guests: lunch time, coffee breaks, maybe whilst they were viewing the products or maybe joining in with training or a practical activity.

- In the gallery – a key position for Joanne would be in the gallery: where she could observe how the day was going and be available to step forward should the need arise. We discussed the pinch points of the day, the critical success moments when Joanne should be on hand and ready to step in if required to support a team member (more on this in chapter 11, about the role of Co-Participator).

- In the kitchen – with so much activity on the day, it would be essential for Joanne to get some time in the kitchen, time to reflect on how the day was going, check in with team members and spend time out of the limelight.

This might include doing some tasks behind the scenes to keep things running smoothly while the team were involved with the open day.

The four positions gave Joanne a way to think about her own role on the day and where best to spend her time to ensure she was adding value whilst stepping back to allow the team to run the day. She now had a picture of the different options, the value of each, and some ideas about when to move from one position to another. She was also more confident that she and the team could be assured that they would catch any unexpected event, while having confidence that they could deliver on the day.

Here's how Joanne used the ideas:

Firstly, she immediately spent time **in the kitchen** using her coaching time with Helen to think through her concerns about the day. She followed this up with a coaching session with each of her team individually to go through their session and their concerns and then as a group where they shared tips from their individual coaching as well as their fears. Noticing how different things were affecting each  person helped with perspective and mutual support. The final outcome of her time in the kitchen was to draw up a contingency plan.

There were a number of different elements planned for the day. One was a practical activity, testing a product which was done in pairs. As each pair went to do the activity, Joanne mingled with the rest of the group gathering useful feed-back – a good opportunity for some **with the guests** time.

Of course Joanne had her own time in the spotlight, but spent much of the day **in the gallery**. She had considered her pinch points in advance and made sure she was on hand at those times. One particular pinch point was the safety briefing at the beginning of the day. Safety is very important as there are hazards on site, and this part of the day had to be handled effectively and yet engagingly. One of the team was very nervous about being filmed while presenting her theory  session, so when the film crew appeared Joanne was by her side to support her. She also noticed from the gallery that nobody had thought to top up the tea and coffee ready for the break. Joanne could step forward so that everyone still got a drink.

Another key **in the kitche**n time for Joanne was at lunch time. Having ensured everyone was served with lunch, she took herself away for 10 minutes. This time really helped Joanne to find her feet again for the afternoon. She was already so proud of the team ... but, there were practical sessions still to come.

The day was a great success and so further events were scheduled. Joanne said: 'the four positions made such a difference to the day. I was much more conscious and confident of what was happening throughout the day and that whatever happened we could sort it.'

Reflective questions

Where would be a good place to move to right now? These questions are designed to get you making the most of opportunities in each of the four positions.

In the spotlight:

- What are your intentions for this time?

- How will you warm up? Even a little will help.

- What might be your first line? (Think about this now; be prepared to revise at the time.)

- When will it be time to step back again?

With the guests:

- Who are the "guests" in your setting? Your team? Customers? Other stakeholders?

- Think of three different occasions in the next two weeks when you can spend time with people from different groups, in an informal and equal setting.

- What will you be interested to ask them?

- How will you stop yourself from simply telling them about how busy/interesting/in demand you are?

In the gallery:

- Select a person/event/situation you'd like to take a closer look at...

- Where could you put yourself to get a useful view from the gallery?

- Pick a time over the next two weeks to go there, and see what you see.

- Who else might you take with you as a "spotter," to help examine the view and give another perspective?

In the kitchen:

- What are you already doing that gives you a little time in the kitchen?

- Which of these is most beneficial to you? How can you do more of it?

- Think of one new thing for which you'd like to try to get some kitchen time, and make a time to try it out in the next month.

Key points

➢ Host Leaders spend their time in four positions:

    ○ In the spotlight – being the focus of attention, out front, making things happen
    ○ With the guests – still out front, but being "one of the group" – not the center of attention
    ○ In the gallery – standing back, taking an overview of what's happening
    ○ In the kitchen – in a more private and intimate space, preparing and reflecting

➢ Moving smoothly between these positions helps us to keep a great all-round perspective on what is happening, so we can step forward when needed and then step back into another position – always alert.

Part Two

Six Roles of Engagement

6

Initiator

> "If you see your path laid out in front of you – Step one, Step two, Step three – you only know one thing ... it is not your path. Your path is created in the moment of action.
>
> If you can see it laid out in front of you, you can be sure it is someone else's path. That is why you see it so clearly."
>
> ~Joseph Campbell[1]

 Initiators get things going. That sounds so obvious it's hardly worth mentioning ... We step forward and decide, somehow, that we want to go somewhere, do something, move on. Simple ...

Or is it? These things don't normally come out of thin air. We respond to the world around us. So these moments of initiating come from experience, from a reaction to something, from dissatisfaction or anger with how things are, or a desire that things should be better tomorrow.

In this chapter, we'll be looking at how initiating is a key role for a Host Leader. Initiating is about getting things started. It's not, however, about then planning the whole journey before we set out. Initiating is about seeing both a worthwhile endeavor and some feasible next steps. Then we can be alert and aware of changing situations and adjust as we go along – a dynamic steering kind of approach. In a volatile, unpredictable, complex and ambiguous (VUCA) world filled with unexpected turns and surprising developments, it's not enough to follow the bland textbook "set goal, make plan, stick to plan, result" thinking. Action, awareness and responsiveness are key.

This powerful idea connects with the Joseph Campbell quote above. Initiating is not the same as having the whole journey planned out in advance. Indeed, if we catch ourselves in that position, we're not really initiating; we're basically following someone else's route or over-planning, maybe micromanaging, or doing the work of others.

We will then go on to consider three stages of the Initiator role:

1. Noticing what's needed – a call to action

2. Getting things started

3. Responding to what happens

and how Initiators constantly move between the three stages. We will start by looking at how the journey can begin and what happens just before that moment.

Noticing what's needed – a call to action

Joseph Campbell's famous work on the *Hero's Journey* story meta-structure[2] gives us a very insightful sense of how "initiating" happens. Campbell examined the ways in which myths and stories are built up, and produced an overlay, an arch structure, by which events often unfold. In Campbell's analysis, stories usually start with a scene-setting section he called "The Ordinary World" – giving us a sense of where and when the events are taking place, and the normal run of things.

Anyone who has sat down with a child at bedtime and told (or even improvised) a story beginning with "Once upon a time…" has been using this starting point. "Once upon a time, there was a little girl named Goldilocks. She went for a walk in the forest. Pretty soon, she came upon a house." Nothing unusual here; it's just normal.

And then, in Campbell's analysis, comes the "Call To Adventure." Something happens that tips the balance out of the ordinary and demands a response. In Goldilocks' case, she knocks on the door and, getting no answer, decides to go in, and finds three bowls of porridge on the table … You know the rest. Had a porridge-eating bear answered the door, we'd have a different story.

The point here is that we rarely initiate entirely on our own, from nothing or out of thin air. There is usually a call to adventure of some kind. This may take the form of an interest, dissatisfaction, a passion, a rage, or just wanting to see something done better or differently. So, when we get mad about something, it may be a call to adventure. Likewise, when we notice ourselves drawn to something, it may be big: end child exploitation or protect wildlife around the world – or it may be smaller: organizing the team's documents so people can find what they need more quickly, or starting to develop a new service line for an ill-served customer group.

Initiating from a call to action

When Mark was working on a previous book, *The Solutions Focus*, he and his co-author were looking for a way to mark the book's publication. They suggested to their Bristol Solutions Group colleagues that, as the solution-focused methodology was starting to creep into coaching and management circles from its therapy homeland, it might be interesting to organize a meeting for anyone interested in this crossover. The group agreed, set a date for a year hence, and booked a small room in a hotel for the meeting. As the year went on and the plans emerged, more people expressed interest, and the expected numbers grew from an initial twenty to forty, then fifty... and finally eighty people attended from nine countries. This group became the SOLWorld community (www.solworld.org), which has subsequently held over thirty international events all over the world.

Changing the focus of a (successful) business

We introduced Derek from Mobysoft in our four positions chapter, with his approach to "in the kitchen" time and the value it brings to him, his business and the team, who provide communication tools for housing associations to interact with their tenants.

The business had reached a level of success and looked set to continue, all based on an SMS-based system where tenants received text messages at certain times. The business plan was built on continuing along the same path. All the signs at the time said *stick with the plan and carry on*.

Then something unexpected happened. A customer realized that Mobysoft's data could help them work with their tenants in a more wide-scale way, with different kinds of messaging and communication. The issues that this helped to solve involved a common problem across social housing associations. By listening to what was needed, Derek noticed two things: customers were calling for a solution to the problem, and new government legislation would make the solution even more valuable. Derek could hear a clear call to reorient the business.

At the time, the original product was used by eighty percent of Mobysoft's customers and represented seventy percent of the revenue, yet it was clear to Derek that the time was right to change direction and take the next steps to develop his new product. This is now the main focus of the business.

Is the call worth answering?

Before starting to get other people involved, there's a key first check that we can do by ourselves: "Am I a customer for change?"

The idea of a "customer for change" has been one of the most powerful developments coming out of the world of solution-focused practice. We may have a hope or dream – but is this the moment to move to some small steps? There are two key criteria by which we can decide whether we are (yet) a customer for change, and therefore in a good place to initiate:

1. We want something to be different

It's important to have something that we want to be different – then we can start things moving in that direction. We have some kind of sense of the direction in which we seek to move – a horizon, in terms of our *User's Guide to the Future*. It may be vague and not very well defined for now – that's totally fine. There are those who would have you define some kind of well-formed outcome as the first step, or some sort of SMART goal. That may turn out to be useful later on, but in Host Leadership terms, we'll probably be wanting to engage others before things get too set in concrete.

2. We are prepared to do something about it now

This second element is even more important. We may want all sorts of things to be different, but there are only so many hours in the day... Having decided what we'd like to be different, we need to pause for a second and ask the question, "Am I prepared to do something about this right now?" We may well not have any idea of what that *something* might be yet... but supposing we had a next step in mind; would we be up for doing it? If the answer is yes, we're a customer for change, and initiating is already underway! Woo-hoo! Now it's just a question of what to do... and we'll be finding all sorts of options appearing in the rest of this book.

This is all about setting an initial direction for our work as leaders. Which way do we want to be going? We can then engage others along the way. This is very coherent with working with an emerging and VUCA world, where unexpected change is normal. The Agile approach to software development and project management is very adept at this kind of "focus with flexibility."

Hearing a call – just one project on time ...

Marcie is the project coordinator at a company manufacturing and then installing hi-tech industrial equipment around the world. Marcie's role is to coordinate all the projects, from orders through to installation and validation. She works alongside a number of project engineers who play a vital role in ensuring projects run smoothly and to plan. She was becoming increasingly frustrated that projects were not going to plan, overrunning on both time and budget, often with remedial work required. Marcie felt powerless to change things and get the project engineers to work with her to improve things.

Helen introduced Marcie to Host Leadership and the six Roles of Engagement, starting with Initiator, asking her, "What one thing would you want to 'initiate' right now? What would be a good first step to sorting how the projects work?" Marcie replied, "One project to go to plan." So Marcie now needed to engage the project team around this one idea.

Helen and Marcie moved on to two other roles: Inviter and Space Creator.

- **Inviter:** Who needs to be involved and why? What are you inviting them to?

  Marcie invited the whole project team to a meeting the following week, saying she'd like to try something different. In the meantime, she gave real thought to how that meeting should run.

- **Space Creator:** Where will you hold the meeting? What kind of space do you need for this interaction?

Everybody came along to the meeting not knowing what to expect yet intrigued. The theme for the meeting was "Mission Possible" and Marcie realized her role was to set the ball rolling then step back and watch what everybody had to offer. She stepped back, nervously. She'd set a ball rolling down hill... but it wasn't totally her party. Marcie had created the space and generated intrigue, done just enough to get it started, but not overprescribed.

Having engaged the whole team with the idea of how each person played a part in projects going to plan, they then worked with a new project, creating the project plan together and what a difference it made! The first project in months went to plan and the format of the project meetings was changed. The old project engineers meetings didn't work; no one wanted to come and projects weren't going to plan. Mission Possible has become "Avengers Assemble" and an "assemble meeting" happens every time there is a new project.

Marcie has realized she is a Host Leader; she hosts the projects and the project team.

Goals and targets

"Plans are only good intentions unless they immediately degenerate into hard work."

~Peter Drucker

We saw in the previous chapter that a responsive and flexible Host Leader will learn to hold lightly their ideas about what exactly the future will bring. By all means set a goal or target as a motivational process – to get this thing done by that date. Targets which are stretching but doable can serve to engage people around a high-profile happening.

The key to success lies not in the target, however, but in what the target does right now. Simply setting a goal, whether it is for a huge topic such as climate change, or a more local affair such as fundraising or sales, is counterproductive if it doesn't turn directly into hard work.

Having heard a call and decided that it's worth answering (at least to start with), we can get things started.

Getting things started

Small steps are not designed to solve whole difficult issues. In our Host Leadership role of Initiator, however, they have enormous power. They allow us to make a move, to start the ball rolling – and then see if the ball rolls like we had anticipated, who else is interested, whether the ball stops or not... actual feedback from the world, rather than from our imagination in trying to plan what might happen (as opposed to seeing what *does* happen).

Mark has been working with small steps as a route to tackling big issues for over twenty years in his work on the Solutions Focus approach.[3] We are constantly amazed at the power of small steps to engage people into action. Solutions Focus offers a whole philosophy and approach to change in people, with a multitude of ways to use the various tools and techniques – but it's small steps that SF users say again and again are the most powerful part of the compendium.

Finding a great small step: Bob Geldof, Band Aid and Live Aid

Anyone who was around in 1985 remembers Live Aid. On July 13th of that year, the two biggest gigs in rock music history were held simultaneously in London and Philadelphia to raise money for famine relief in Ethiopia. A vast array of stars performed, and 1.9 billion people watched the live TV relays in 150 countries, making this the most-watched event at the time. A total of $140 million was raised.[4]

The Live Aid event sprang from the Band Aid singles *Do They Know It's Christmas?* and *We Are The World*, which also used big all-star lineups to get attention and raise money for Ethiopia. Many people will recall that Irish punk singer Bob Geldof was a driving force behind all of these happenings, and that his attention was caught by a shocking BBC news report on the famine victims. But what happened next? Did he instantly know what to do next? No, he didn't. This is an interesting case of looking around for a great next step.

Geldof lay awake thinking about the awful situation, replaying the images in his mind. What to do? Send money. Of course, but that didn't seem enough. Anyway, at the time, Geldof was down on his luck, having released a series of records which had flopped. Donate the profits of his next record? On current form, that would be a pitiful amount, but it would be more than he alone could give. He slept fitfully.

The following morning, Geldof went to his record company's offices to help to promote the next record. As he tried to focus on phoning sales offices around the country, everything seemed irrelevant compared to the disaster unfolding in Africa. He recalled later:

> *"Yesterday it had seemed desperately important. Now it seemed meaningless. I tentatively suggested I was thinking of doing a record for the Ethiopians to the four people in the press office. 'Yeah, you should,' said Bernadette. 'I saw it last night, it was awful,' said Mariella. 'What kind of record?' said Steve."*[5]

They hadn't laughed – they liked the idea. But what kind of record? Geldof phoned his wife Paula Yates, who was recording the music TV show *The Tube*, and told her that he was thinking of asking some other people to get involved to improve potential sales. Who else was on the show and therefore hanging around in the TV studio that week? Midge Ure of the band Ultravox – who was an old friend. He agreed at once, *AND* he had an outline that might be developed into a suitable song. Encouraged, Geldof called Sting (The Police) and Simon Le Bon (Duran Duran). They were both keen, and Geldof set about contacting other leading musicians. It was only at the end of the day, after more calls and chance encounters with Gary and Martin Kemp from Spandau Ballet, that the idea formed that the more people who were on the record, the better it could do in money-raising terms.

And it went from there. *Do They Know It's Christmas?* sold over six million copies; *We Are The World* nearly ten million. Geldof heard a call, and heard it very clearly. He also (perhaps unconsciously) recognized a good small step – one which leads to something else, something bigger. He spoke to those around him; he invited close friends to be involved. We see the whole Band Aid/Live Aid saga as a great example of leading as a host.

Small steps into smaller steps

One thing we have noticed over the years is that some people's ideas of what makes a small step need a little refinement. For us, as Initiators, a small step might be defined as follows:

- Can be done in the next day or two (at most)

- Can be done without getting the go-ahead from anyone else

- Makes excellent sense to you as a next step

We often find that people are used to starting their thinking at a "quite big step" level; for example, someone might decide that a small step towards moving their business forward is: "Redo my whole marketing plan!"

That's a step, possibly a useful step, but almost certainly not a small step. So, we deploy the secret weapon to make the step smaller by asking, "And what would be a small step towards that?"

The answer to this may be smaller – for example, "Look at the marketing data for the last three months?"

"And what would be a small step towards that?"

"Get hold of the data…"

And again: "Ask Frank to get the Web stats, ask Amy to bring in the sales figures, invite them and Joanna to a meeting to look at what's working at the moment."

Aha – we finally have some small steps that meet the target criteria above – they can be done in a day or two at most, and don't need anyone else to okay them and get things moving.

Notice that some of the small steps are about inviting other people to be involved. This happens a lot in our experience, and we will be looking at the Host Leadership role of Inviter – engaging people with the soft power of invitation – in the next chapter.

So we've seen how the role of Initiator involves:

- Listening to what's being called for

- Getting things moving

- Having a long-term hope/goal/dream

- And small steps in the right direction

We could be thinking that initiating is only about starting things and that once they're started, that's the Initiator done. However, in reality, the Initiator is ongoing. Hosts, and Host Leaders, keep listening to what's being called for.

Responding to what happens

A key skill for Host Leaders is to be aware of what's happening so we can respond to it. This is the counterpart to small steps – a small step sets things in motion, other things happen, which allow us to take another small (as big as feels comfortable and confident) step. Sometimes these steps will clearly be the next step along the way to our longer-term hopes. Other times, there will be unexpected events to be included, used, or stepped around. These might require modest adjustments, or perhaps a "deep-breath moment" of reassessment.

Stepping back to notice

Let us think about stepping forward and back. When we take action, this is usually done by stepping forward. Responding to what happens, on the other hand, often starts with stepping back.

Good hosts and Host Leaders can do this from time to time – perhaps by being "In the gallery" or even taking a moment "In the kitchen." A quick breath and an overview give an idea of what is happening, how things are going, and what needs to happen next. This process of proceeding "a breath at a time" is sometimes called the *chaordic* path – the border of order and chaos, with each step emerging from the last.

Focusing on what's working

It can be very tempting to focus on what hasn't gone well, but a key logic of our *User's Guide to the Future* goes like this: it's the things that *help* that will move you along, not the things that *hinder*. Often we find that people are content to simply accept the things that are helping, and focus their energy on trying to sort out the interfering factors. So, here is the best question to ask when you are reviewing progress and looking to adjust.

What's better?

Just that: what progress have we made, and how? This question really makes great use of dynamic steering. We are not simply looking for what we achieved that was expected. We are not looking at the success of our small steps. We are looking for progress – from *any* source. That includes unexpected events, strokes of luck, useful synchronicity, random happenings and anything else.

This is where the "tiny signs of progress" come in useful. If we know the tiny signs of progress we are hoping for, we are more easily equipped to see them, notice them and respond to them. Also, lack of progress in a certain area may not be a disaster – it may be a question of timing, it may mean we need to refocus on that aspect, or it may mean that particular thing is no longer as relevant as it once was.

A good sequence of questions to review and build on progress might therefore look like this:

1. What's better? (Make a big list; keep asking "What else?")

2. Has the overall direction shifted? Quickly reassess the horizon for any changes.

3. What's next? More small steps, building on and adding to what has worked so far.

As a host, we may be responding very rapidly to developing situations. Lots of things will crop up that need small responses, without necessitating a big rethink. However, there are times when we become aware that things have shifted to such an extent that it's time for a new focus. We call such times a deep-breath moment.

Hosting around the world: Keeping going for British jazz at Ronnie Scott's

Ronnie Scott was a British tenor saxophonist bewitched by modern jazz. In the 1940s, he had worked his passage on the liners to New York to see the giants of bebop perform in the clubs around 52nd Street, and came back filled with a desire to have something similar in London – a place where young adventurous UK musicians could perform their edgy music without being booed off by unhappy diners, and where the best American stars could perform to a sympathetic audience. He finally raised £1000 with his colleague Peter King and opened in the basement of 39 Gerrard Street, Soho in 1959.

The club was a success, and attracted the musicians and audiences that Scott had envisaged (though they had to fight a union ban on visiting Americans to make it happen). A generation of British players grew up around the scene, with Zoot Sims, Sonny Rollins, Bill Evans and many more taking up residencies. Rollins liked the atmosphere of the club so much that he asked to be locked in overnight while he worked on the music for the 1966 film *Alfie*, starring Michael Caine. During the 1960s, the club moved to bigger premises in Frith Street, where it remains to this day. Despite being in perpetual financial trouble, Scott and King managed, by hook or by crook, to keep going. Scott died in 1999, but his name and spirit live on – the club still runs late-night sessions of the kind that inspired him in New York. Ronnie Scott was a good tenor saxophonist, but is remembered throughout the jazz world as a brave and persistent Initiator who managed to adjust, keep going and maintain a special place for British musicians.

Making big adjustments – the "deep-breath moment"

Good hosting is always adaptive. Even though we may know what we'd like to happen next, it doesn't always end up that way. Extra people may show up, dietary requirements change and accidents happen. Host Leadership is just the same. A good host (and a good Host Leader) knows when to step back and take a deep breath.

This isn't just any old bump in the road. There are times when what's emerging is getting to be at odds with what we intended. A poor Host Leader will not notice – they just keep driving towards the original goals. This is usually because they are not looking at what's happening, because they "know" already. A good Host Leader, on the other hand, will sense that things are coming to the point where a rethink is required.

The first thing to say is that this is not a sign of bad planning. On the contrary; it's a sign that the *User's Guide to the Future* is being used well. One of the wonders of viewing the world as emergent is to acknowledge that the unexpected will sometimes happen, and that's just how it is. The key thing is not to totally prevent the unexpected (which would be futile) but to respond to it well and to use it constructively.

Sir Chris Bonington – awareness on Everest

Everest mountaineer Sir Chris Bonington led many expeditions into the highest and most dangerous mountains in the world. He sums up the need for responsiveness very well. He says:

"The clear vision is important – then you keep pressing on, or indecision takes place. Of course you have to be prepared to change plans – it's a balance. Be inflexible and drive on into trouble, be a ditherer and get nowhere. You have to get the balance right."

Chris told us of his experience leading an expedition to the South West face of Mount Everest in 1975. This route was very much "the hard way" to ascend the world's highest peak – five expeditions had already tried and failed, including one led by Bonington in 1972. The climb had broadly gone well, and Bonington was enjoying taking his turn out at the front, forging the route. (Ascents on great peaks such as Everest involve groups of climbers taking turns to make the route, descend to a lower camp to rest and acclimatize to the altitude, and then carry supplies up to their colleagues.) It seemed as if the expedition might succeed way beyond expectations. Then, in conversation with expedition doctor Charlie Clarke, came a deep-breath moment. Bonington recalls:

"I had been at 8000 m altitude for ten days. I'd planned out a third summit bid (as well as the two already planned) with bigger groups and myself taking part in the third summit bid, so we could double the number of people getting to the summit, not for a record but so that as many people as possible could enjoy the satisfaction – it was technically feasible. I was fine. Then Charlie pointed out over the walky-talky that I would have had to have stayed for another five days – which would have been too much. AND there were a lot of unhappy climbers at the bottom who had not

been included in the summit bids. I was on the radio to them, but it's a terse medium ... I had been at the right place [high up] at Camp 5 supervising and taking part in the push through the Rock Band. Once I had nominated the summit bids, there was nothing more for me to do there. So, nominating someone else for the third summit bid and going back down to help sort things at Advance Base was the right thing..."

The expedition succeeded in getting Doug Scott and Dougal Haston to the summit in the first bid, and Peter Boardman and Pertemba Sherpa in the second, albeit with the loss of climbing cameraman Mick Burke who disappeared after pushing on alone during the second summit ascent. This was the second of Bonington's three expeditions to Everest as leader. He did not make the summit himself on any of these. He did finally succeed in making it to the top –as a "guest" and logistics planner on Norwegian Arne Naess's 1985 expedition, rather than as the host of his own efforts.

The unexpected power of not knowing

As leaders, we often think that it's our role to know. To know what to do, to know where we're going, to know how to get there. One refreshing part of Host Leadership is, of course, to embrace another possibility: that of knowing to some extent where we *want* to go – and then to *not know* how to get there, but to start with a good small first step. This is a great example of the way Host Leaders can embrace the dilemmas of modern leadership we mentioned in the opening chapter.

The idea of not knowing comes from Zen philosophy. One good way to consider the power of not knowing is to start with this quote from Zen philosopher Shunryu Suzuki:

> *"In the beginner's mind there are many possibilities; in the expert's mind there are few."*[6]

The expert knows what to do – so that is all they can see. The beginner, on the other hand, knows nothing – so in some ways can attain a view with many more possibilities. This means that in some situations – particularly those which are uncharted, complex, wicked, persistently problematic – the mind of the beginner may be more useful than the mind of the expert (who would presumably have sorted it all out by now if he did, indeed, know what to do). Remember the idea of the *encuentro* – the meeting without explicit purpose, and hence with maximum possibility.

This section is about the deep-breath moment – the moment when you become aware (in the words of Art of Hosting steward Jerry Nagel) that something new is trying to emerge. Jerry calls this the "un-named state" – we can't name it, because we don't really know what it is yet; however, sometimes we become aware that the tide is moving into a new direction around us. This kind of moment is an excellent time to take a deep breath and follow another of our favorite maxims from the In the Gallery position:

"Don't just do something – stand there!"

This is, in the language of Host Leadership, to take a big step back. We want for a moment to stop, observe, experience what is happening. What seems to be emerging here – a new question, a new perspective, a new goal, a new possibility? Think about a time when you've suddenly become aware of a new thought, one that wasn't there before, but has somehow slipped into the room unnoticed. It's almost impossible, in our judgment, to notice the moment such possibilities arrive. However, once they are there, it's usually worth stopping and paying attention to them, even if we subsequently decide not to pursue them for now.

"Standing there," in this case, is not at all the same as "doing nothing." Sometimes we find leaders who are very loath to even look as if they are doing nothing, and therefore do everything they can *not* to – which means never stepping back, never pausing, never stopping to smell the flowers and see what might be emerging right next to them.

Stepping back

 At the end of each Role chapter, we will look at when to step back from that role, to assess the situation and think about our next moves. So, think about when to step back from the role of Initiator. To start with, it all seems to be about stepping forward – to see a future hope, to act with a great and positive intention, to find some small next steps, to step in just before things are required.

In this last part of the chapter, however, we have also seen how the Initiator's role is sometimes to step back – to take stock, to check in, to sometimes nudge things in the right direction. And – possibly most importantly of all – to take a deep breath and sense that something new is emerging. Because that is the moment when a new hope can appear, a new intention be forged, and Initiating can begin once more.

Initiator

- Listen for what is being called for
- Avoid "ant country"
- Keep awareness of what's happening
- Form a hope, dream or intention
- Get things moving – small steps
- Respond with dynamic steering

Reflective questions

- What is calling you to action right now – in your work, at home, in your community?

- What would be a great hope, dream or intention to pursue for you?

- What would be the benefit of that – for you, for others, for society?

- What would be a great first step towards that? What else? What could you do in the next 24 hours?

- What would be the first tiny signs of progress for you? And who else might notice?

- When do you take the chance to step back, take a deep breath, and reflect?

Key Points

> The Initiator role is about getting things moving in a useful, productive or necessary direction.

> Listen for what is being called for – and choose whether to accept that call.

> Employ the *User's Guide to the Future* to help align your hopes, intentions and actions.

> Don't make detailed plans from day one; rather, focus on small actions to get things moving, which will also engage others and provide you with feedback.

> Use dynamic steering to keep adjusting and making progress by embracing unexpected change rather than fighting it or attempting to eliminate it.

> Keep awareness of what is emerging, and be prepared to take a deep breath from time to time and reconsider.

7

Inviter

"If I can attract you to want to do what I want you to do, then I do not have to force you to do what you do not want to do."

~Prof Joseph Nye

 It would be very strange to find someone roaming the streets demanding that passersby come to their house for dinner, wouldn't it? That's because a fundamental quality of the host (and the Host Leader) is *inviting,* not *insisting.* As you will see in this chapter, the power of invitation stretches way beyond simple requests, right into the heart of human relationships. And we can use it in all kinds of situations, whether we are in a position to "invite" people or not.

Thinking invitationally

Anyone can be a Host Leader at any level of an organization. If you manage staff, you're a leader. If you engage with customers, you're a leader. If you engage with stakeholders, you're a leader. If you engage with the public, you're a leader (in their eyes anyway). But we may be thinking that we can't go around issuing invitation cards to anyone and everyone. Of course not. But we CAN think invitationally.

Thinking invitationally is at the heart of Host Leadership. When we invite, and people accept, they show up being involved, open, engaged, part of the process. When we invite, and people don't accept, well, that's a message from the universe that what we're offering isn't exactly what is wanted. More on that later.

Thinking invitationally is about reaching out and engaging with those around us in a way which invites – rather than insists – that they join us in working on some project, purpose or endeavor. It's about seeing the participation of others as a valuable gift, rather than the result of a contract of employment. (There may well be a contract of employment, but if you get to the point of insisting on the terms of that to achieve participation, well, you should have read this book sooner.)

Giving choice and space

The Inviter dimension of Host Leadership is about using the soft power of invitation and influence. "Soft power" has been identified by Professor Joseph Nye of Harvard University as the key developing strand at the level of international relations and diplomacy. Nye contrasts soft power with hard power. Hard power is already familiar to us – the power of force and coercion.[1]

The idea of soft power is a new thing in the workplace – part of the humanization of the world of work – and fits the host metaphor well. As we will see in this chapter, there are many practical and small ways to use soft power, whatever your formal position. We will be considering stepping forward with invitational thinking – using soft power in large, but mostly small, practical ways to engage our fellow workmates, colleagues and communities.

As we will see, acting as an Inviter includes the less active (but no less valuable) act of giving people choice and space. When we invite folks around to our house, we don't hassle them for an immediate answer. It's the done thing to give them a chance to think about it (and for very good reason, as we will see). What we lose in time and urgency is repaid many times over in a much more priceless commodity – commitment.

Hard and soft power

Hard power is usually based on an ability to produce negative consequences. "Do this – or else …" power. This kind of power is not going away anytime soon, of course. However, we are coming to realize that this is not a very productive source of power on its own. For one, it assumes that the coerced will remain in a position not to retaliate – which may not always be the case, and then the revolution comes. More generally, hard power tends to get minimum compliance – people do what's asked/expected of them, and no more. What's more, they usually do it grudgingly and without spirit or charm. Hard power is not good for positive and productive relationship building. It demands a compliant and obedient pose from the followers.

Soft power, on the other hand, is usually about potential positive consequences. An outstretched hand, inviting participation in something good. An influence, rather than an order. This is nothing new – indeed, the power of positive influence, like hosting, is as old as humanity. When we are offered a choice, however, the tone is set for a participative relationship – not based on subjugation and power but on cooperation and mutual interaction. One of the key benefits of soft power is that it builds relationships for greater things to come, rather than achieving a limited quick action at the cost of relational capital.

Smart power – soft and hard

Nye is clear that soft power is not wholly the answer. He defines a synthesis, "smart power," as the ability to combine hard and soft power to achieve results. Occasionally, soft power isn't enough, and hard-power tactics are required. More often in everyday settings, the relationships built with soft power allow the odd instance of more direct approaches to be incorporated without too much in the way of negative consequence.

Former CEO of GE Jeff Immelt has related his experience of running this huge corporation. He is quoted as saying,[2] "There are seven to twelve times a year when you have to say, 'You're doing it my way.' If you do it eighteen times, the good people will leave. If you do it three times, the company falls apart." Adopting a soft-power approach does not mean never giving an instruction – it does, however, build a much better basis for the occasional firm steer.

The smart-power matrix

Smart power is the combined used of soft and hard power. We can think of these different options using this four-box matrix.

Those who are mainly focused on results use hard-power tactics. Those who are more focused on relationships may be more open to soft-power moves like inviting and involving. However, an awareness of both and when to use them brings the possibility of smart power. The great benefit of smart power, as we saw above, is that the relationships which are built with soft power make it a good deal easier to insist occasionally without seriously damaging the relationships.

The fourth box in the smart-power matrix is an interesting one. It looks like someone with no power. Actually, it represents the people who have power and influence – but are not yet using it. Perhaps someone who has not taken a look at their potential influence lately, someone who is coasting a bit, someone who feels drawn to a call to action but has yet to look around for others to engage. A great advantage of soft power is that it doesn't require conventional levers like money, authority or position. Rather, it stems from building relationships, developing connections, making the first moves, reaching out. So, look around you and think about how you might use your soft power more effectively.

The concept of hosting is a great way to build your soft power. It is also a route to using whatever authority and position you have in a context of positive relationships, which builds effectiveness and results. So, if you are reading this and feeling that you have an idea, passion or concern which is not getting the notice it deserves, then maybe you are the one to host it.

In terms of individual relations, soft power is fortunately a much more natural process – at least in society in general. As we will see in this chapter, there are many practical and small ways to use soft power, whatever your formal position. We will be considering stepping forward with invitational thinking – using soft power in large, but mostly small, practical ways to engage our fellow workmates, colleagues and communities.

Three aspects of powerful invitation

"An invitation is always an acknowledgment."

Lynne Twist, co-founder of the Pachamama Alliance

An okay invitation will give information and request you participate. A really powerful invitation, however, will contain elements of three aspects: acknowledgement, attraction and choice.

Acknowledgement – What I value about *YOU* and why I'd really like you to be part of this.

Think about it: to receive a great invitation is always affirming. Even if we don't want to say yes, it's an honor to have been asked. It just feels good to be invited; the experience of an invitation is nourishing. In the context of leadership, leaders can always invite people into a conversation. And then the people feel seen – acknowledged. An invitation says, "I see you. You are there. You are unique. I want you with me. You are just the right person for this project/time/event/moment." Even if you don't want to play, you feel seen.

A key part of this acknowledgment is to focus on what you appreciate about the person, their skills, qualities, strengths – why is it that we want *them* to be with us? We can think of this as "affirming" – offering our perception of useful personal qualities. This is a powerful tool in its own right, as Mark's previous work on Solutions Focus has shown.

Attraction – To what am I inviting you?

Secondly, an invitation needs to be attractive. What's the project? What are our best hopes, intentions, vision, purpose, objectives? What will the benefits be, and who will enjoy/reap them? When well executed, invitations connect with the person's vision of themselves, honor it and match it with the project, the conversation, the opportunity. We find the center point in them and the hopes, intentions and direction for our project and make that connection.

We have seen how to build the direction of our projects in the chapter on the Initiator dimension. As an Inviter, we will be wanting to think about how to connect specifically with those whom we wish to engage.

Choice – to get an authentic and heartfelt Yes, there has to be the possibility of a No.

Third, an invitation has choice. For there to be the possibility of a meaningful Yes, there also has to be the possibility of an equally meaningful No. As the inviter, it can pay to not be too attached to the outcome of this particular invitation. Of course, we are hoping for an affirmative and positive answer – but a No, particularly if it's a "positive No" (coming up in the Gatekeeper chapter), can also be very useful. It has to be (somewhat) okay if the person says no, because then there IS the space and the grace to say Yes.

If there is no possibility of a No, then it's not an invitation – it's an order. There may be times for orders, but they are not the best way to get things off the ground.

A not very compelling invitation

During the writing of this book, Mark received this invitation:

> *I am a committee member on the Manchester committee of the ABC Institute. I am looking for speakers on solution-focused performance management to speak to our members on November 21ˢᵗ, six-thirty p.m. start – eight p.m. end. I was wondering if it is something you would be interested in doing.*

> *We will advertise the event to our five thousand members through newsletters, social media accounts, website and printed program booklet. I operate on a limited budget; therefore I cannot pay fees or expenses.*

> *I look forward to your reply.*

Manchester is four hours' drive from Mark's home in London. There are no fees or expenses. They know exactly what they want; there is no flexibility. Let us look at this through the lens of a great invitation:

Acknowledgement: He is asking for a topic on which Mark is a world expert; however, there is no mention of why it's *him* they want, what in particular about his work is important, how they settled on this topic as being important, or how they are keen on his work.

Attractive: No fees or expenses. No mention of any form of welcome, meal, interesting crowd, exclusivity of the group, previous notable speakers, how it might be useful to *Mark* (as opposed to *them*).

Optional: At least there is a choice! However, the choice seems to be to broadly accept or not...

There is a postscript to this particular tale: the organizer later phoned Mark, and with some instant coaching based around a "positive No", he was able to make his offer considerably more compelling.

Now let us look at a *really* compelling invitation.

An invitation from the president: should I stay or should I go?

Having been in prison for twenty-seven years, Nelson Mandela was finally elected as the first black president of South Africa on April 27, 1994. The following morning, his first day in office, Mandela arrived at the presidential offices to find the security team packing their bags. Having been hired by the outgoing white President FW de Klerk, they assumed that Mandela would wish to replace them with his own, probably black, staff.

John Reinders was in the president's office. Mandela arrived and asked him where he was going. Reinders replied that he would be returning to his previous position in correctional services (the prison system).

> *"Mandela said, 'I would like you to consider staying here with us.' Reinders was astonished. Mandela continued, 'Yes, I am quite serious. You know this job. I don't. I am from the bush. I am ignorant. Now, if you stay with me, it would be just one term, that is all. Five years. And then, of course, you would be free to leave. Now, please understand me: this is not an order. I would like to have you here only if you wish to stay and share your knowledge and your experience with me. So, what do you say? Will you stay with me?' Reinders did not hesitate.*
>
> *Then Mandela asked Reinders to gather all the presidential staff – including the cleaners, gardeners, and everyone else, in the Cabinet room for a meeting. He walked among them, shaking hands, exchanging a few words (in Afrikaans where appropriate, having learned it in prison). Then he addressed them. 'Hello, I'm Nelson Mandela. If any of you prefer to take the [severance] package, you are free to leave. Go. There is no problem. But, I beg you, stay! Five years, that is all. You have the knowledge. We need that knowledge, we need that experience of yours.' Every single member of the Presidential staff stayed."[3]*

This remarkable story shows all three elements of a powerful invitation in action:

Acknowledgement: *"You know this job; you've been doing it for years. In fact you know it much better than me."*

Attraction: *"I want you to share your knowledge and experience with me, so we can build a new and better country for all, whatever their color. And I am showing this desire by extending this invitation to you now. And it's just for five years, not for ever, so you can see longer-term possibilities beyond that."*

Choice: *"You are free to go if you wish; that's fine. Indeed, there is a severance package on the table right now. It's up to you."*

"But I inherited my team – I can't invite them ..."

One of the most common responses we get when presenting Host Leadership to managers in organizations is, "This sounds fantastic! However, I already have my team, I can't invite them." Well, yes, you can. That's why this section is called "Thinking invitationally."

What we can do is start to engage your team around new priorities, ideas, focus on customers or stakeholders, or whatever else are the key priorities. You can even engage them in a conversation about what the key priorities are, right now. You can offer alternatives rather than ultimatums. You can seek participation rather than submission. Mark recalls being very critical of his manager's lack of action about future plans during his time in the electricity industry. He was rewarded with an invitation from the manager to lead the development of the selfsame plans – an offer which could not really be refused. Invitation is about clearing a space in front of people, rather than trying to push them into it.

Invitational language

As a Host Leader, you will want to be watching your language closely. Mark remembers an activity during a management course early in his career where he was set the challenge to engage with a "difficult staff member" without recourse to veiled threats ("If you don't do this, then bad things will happen") and failed miserably. Over the years, he has learned how to engage with people in a more positive and constructive way, which means taking care with language.

Invitational language invites people to consider something, while leaving open other possibilities. If there are no other possibilities, it's not an invitation; it's an instruction. This is quite a subtle business. While it is difficult to offer hard and fast rules (which do not in any case reflect the complexities of life and language), we can share some general guidelines.

Inviting or subjugating?

We can draw a basic distinction between inviting language/gestures and subjugating language/gestures. *Inviting* means holding out a hand of engagement, looking for a constructive response. *Subjugating* means using hard power to demand acceptance, without flexibility.[4] A good host will look to invite people into discussion about how to achieve targets, even if the target is not negotiable (perhaps by coming from a non-hosting boss). A simple example to start with, from the world of target setting:

Inviting	Subjugating
We're looking to sell more widgets in the third quarter. Your team sold 1000 in that period last year – how many do you think your team could do, given good support?	We need to sell more widgets in the third quarter – your team's target is 1200. Your bonus depends on meeting this target.

The inviting example offers a start to a conversation. The subjugating example only offers two responses – either Yes (in which the leader's figure is accepted), or No (in which case we now have the beginnings of a conflict). Of course, a smart responder could find a way to make something constructive out of the second example, but the leader isn't making life easy in terms of the way they have phrased the initial statement.

Questions or statements

The example above shows another feature of invitational language – phrasing things as a question, rather than a statement. A question automatically invites an answer. A statement just is – and is there either to be accepted or challenged.

Question	Statement
How could we make 10% efficiency savings in next year's budget?	You have to reduce next year's budget by 10%.

People's natural response to a question, at least one that is well put, is to seek to answer it. That's how conversations work – one person says something and the other responds into the space created by the first (and so on). So, asking a question invites a response that builds on the question. (Of course, it may not always get one – but we are moving the possibilities in our favor.)

The example above also shows another key way to use invitational language.

Inclusive language or individual language

Using "we" in a question implies that this is a joint effort – something that all of us will be doing together. So, using "we" in the statement above foreshadows that this is a collective exercise, with input being sought widely. The counterpart using "you" says that this is your problem, not mine. While this might be part of an attempt to delegate, it can come across as subjugating and excluding. Host Leaders co-participate, so will look to use inclusive language wherever possible. Here is another example:

Inclusive	Individual
We need to tackle a problem that affects all of us in the department.	Your behavior over the past months has reached a point I can no longer tolerate.

The inclusive version puts us all in it together. The individual version clearly points fingers of blame and responsibility, which may be tempting… but what kind of response does this invite? Either a submission ("Okay, I'll try to do better") or more likely a fight ("Well, look at *yourself*, you bullying ****!").

Soft language or hard language

Sometimes leaders think that being very clear is a necessary part of leadership. This can sometimes be the case – but it is frequently not a way to invite participation and engagement. Using "softeners" in our language can make it much easier for others to join the conversation and express their views in ways which contribute but don't challenge authority. Here is an example:

Soft	Hard
It would be helpful if you could look at this report today – I'd like to include your input. Is that possible?	Look at this report today. Tomorrow is too late.

The soft version invites a response. The hard version invites acceptance – or else. There are lots of softeners in English, which is a language in which these tactics are used *quite* often (see what we did there…). In addition to "quite," examples of softeners include:

- I wonder if... *(and you can help me decide)*

- There is a slight problem with... *(not a big problem, so we can look into dealing with it together rather than looking for blame)*

- Maybe we should do this... *(and again you are encouraged to give me your thoughts)*

- This might be a good strategy... *(and again it might not, so please say what you think)*

This is an area where there are considerable cultural differences about what is accepted around the world. Some cultures (like the Dutch, for example) pride themselves on being direct and treat bold statements as quite normal. In other places, such as Japan, there are all kinds of ways to hint at what you think, which need decoding to get the message (and if you are Japanese, you will know the code). However, the basic principle of softer language being more inviting is broadly applicable.

Positive language or negative language

The last distinction we will make in this section is the difference between using positive or negative language. Let's look at a simple distinction between problems and solutions.

Positive	Negative
When does the team work at its best together?	When does the team work really badly together?

In engineering logic, these are the same questions asked in different directions – what makes something go up must be the opposite of what makes it come down, so both of the questions will give equivalent answers. If we look at the words, however, we see that the conversations will go in two very different directions.

The positive example will lead to thinking about times when the team works well and what helps that to happen. This in turn tends to produce a positive atmosphere and energy, with people enjoying recalling those times and expanding the discussion, adding more details, encouraging each other, and so on. The negative example will, in contrast, lead to remembering times when things went disastrously, which is depressing and embarrassing, and a conversation which no one really wants to have.

If we are to assume that the purpose of the conversation is to improve team performance (as opposed to beating the team with a stick), the positive conversation will produce more engagement and ideas. See *The Solutions Focus* book[5] for lots more on this topic.

Hosting around the world: What time is when?

One area where hosting traditions differ around the world is the time when one is expected to arrive. In the USA, an invitation for eight p.m. means pretty much just that – arrive at eight p.m. or soon after. Just across the border in Mexico, however, only a fool would show up at eight p.m. with such an invitation – the party would start at ten p.m., eleven p.m., or even later. In Belgium, party invitations sometimes come with a brief timetable about what will happen when – unthinkable in Brazil, for example.

Traditions about when the party is over also differ widely. In the USA, the host may call an end to proceedings and invite their guests to leave. In Mexico, this would be a very unusual situation! In the UK, wedding celebrations tend to be rather open-ended affairs, running on late into the night and gradually tailing off. In China, the guests leave promptly after the speeches and banquet have finished.

The power of the ask

> *"When we don't use the 'Power of the Ask,' we are in essence saying 'No' before the question has even been asked."*
>
> Deborah Mills-Scofield[6]

The "power of the ask" is a well-known expression in fundraising circles. Unless we ask, straight out, for money, people are unlikely to give any. Of course, if we just ask without any preamble, you may not get much response. The effectiveness of the ask is closely linked to the relationship we've built (using soft power) and how compelling our story is. If people feel they are going to be part of something really wonderful, they'll give – in terms of time, commitment and effort as well as money.

A key element of thinking invitationally is therefore to remember the power of the ask, and to make sure our invitation is seen clearly as such. Make sure we have an action step for people to accept – and remember, the easier it is to do the action step, the better.

Asking for the (nearly) impossible at Renold

Bob Davies was chief executive of Renold PLC, leaders in chain and gearbox manufacturing, based in Manchester, UK. He tells of difficult times during the downturn of 2008, and how he had to ask for the nearly impossible. Despite good contingency planning, the company's order book just dried up for a time. Davies focused on keeping the company in a position that would enable it to be recoverable when things turned up. This meant asking some tough questions of both staff and suppliers. Staff took a ten percent pay cut. However, the really impossible part was approaching the company's lawyers and accountants – professions with a tradition of looking after their own incomes with an eagle eye. "We went to our lawyers and accountants and said, 'Our sales are down by twenty-five percent – so will you drop your fees by twenty-five percent? – and they said yes straight away!" recalls Davies. He had clearly built a good relationship over the years, and was now in a position to use the power of the ask.

Asking for the moon: A prize for success

The X PRIZE Foundation (xprize.org) offers prizes to bring about radical innovations for the benefit of humanity. The best known of these prizes was probably the Ansari X PRIZE for the first privately funded manned space flight (the $10m was won in 2004 by Scaled Composites for their craft SpaceShipOne). At the time of writing, there are many different prizes for various innovations in the fields of lunar exploration, handheld health diagnosis (a "tricorder," as seen on *Star Trek*), digital health data and the condition of the oceans. These huge challenges invite the attention of thinkers, mavericks, inventors and entrepreneurs from around the world and provide a space where thinking big can be well rewarded.

This is not a new idea, of course. In 1908, the *Daily Mail* newspaper in London offered a huge prize (by the standards of the time) of £1000 for the first person to fly the English Channel. The prize was won the following year by Frenchman

Louis Blériot after his fellow countryman and challenger Hubert Latham was forced to ditch his plane into the sea six miles short of the coast. The whole affair caused a vast amount of public interest in the new-fangled flying, with Blériot becoming an instant celebrity, and prompting the headline: "England is no longer an island."

Even further back, governments sought to engage clever minds on important and apparently insoluble problems with an invitation. The matter of how to calculate longitude and therefore plot a ship's position when out of sight of land was a massive concern for seafarers for centuries. As long ago as 1527, King Philip of Spain offered a prize for the first person to solve the problem (though nobody won, some were offered smaller grants to continue their research). The British Government passed an Act of Parliament in 1714 setting out a range of prizes for increasing accuracy, including a massive top prize of £20,000 (millions of pounds in today's money). The prize was finally won by John Harrison in 1765 – Harrison's marine chronometer was a watch which could keep accurate time for weeks even on a pitching ship, allowing accurate calculations to be made.

British innovation charity Nesta has come to a similar conclusion in announcing a series of challenge prizes, with a big-time antibiotic research "Longitude Prize for the 21st century." British Astronomer Royal Lord Martin Rees said at the time that the idea of offering a prize, rather than simply funding some research, answers a pressing need to channel more brainpower into innovation, to jump-start new technologies, and to enthuse young people.[7]

All these examples show how an invitation – well designed and carefully positioned – can engage people to explore new ideas and invest considerable sums in the hope of being the first to crack a problem or deliver something new. How could *you* engage people to support *you*?

Hosting around the world: Hearing the invitation in Australia

Mark interviewed Garry Creighton, an Aboriginal health education officer from Tamworth, New South Wales, as part of the research for this book. Garry is a Gomeroi (Murri) man, and spoke movingly about both the importance of tradition and land to his people, and his frustration that his ancestors were prevented from practicing their traditional way of life and were forcibly removed from their tribal lands upon white settlement. Garry told us of the importance of finding out about one's host in advance. "When I go somewhere, I always do my research – who are the Elders, what are the traditions; find out what to do, what to acknowledge verbally at a gathering."

At the end of the phone interview, Garry invited Mark to come and meet him in his home town. "One day when you are out this way, I wouldn't mind sitting down for a coffee with you and we can talk further." Mark was at the end of his trip to Australia and so mentally filed this in the "sometime" category. It was only later that he realized that Garry had made an understated but very important gesture. By offering to continue the conversation, Garry was perhaps making the biggest offer he could – to carry on and build the relationship, to keep exploring together. Coming from busy London, where "we must have lunch" means precisely the opposite, it wasn't easy to hear the significance of the invitation. Having a next step in the diary – another meeting, a next opportunity – means that things are continuing to develop. If there is no next step, then it's much harder work to resuscitate the relationship to make more progress. Can you hear the offer of a next step? How can you make such offers in ways that can be heard by others?

Giving choice and space

"Empowered followers empower leaders." ~Joseph Nye[8]

If stepping forward is to think invitationally and be active in engaging people, then we will also need to become adept at the partner aspect of this dimension – giving space and choice. Why might we do this? After all, we want to take the lead – right? As with all the aspects of Host Leadership, this is about dancing forward and back. These two aspects together create far more powerful leadership than either one of them on its own.

Stepping back invites others to act

Accepting an invitation brings responsibility and commitment for the "guest" too. So, we have to allow some thinking time for the invitees to consider how this invitation sits for them and how they wish to respond. When the response comes, it's heartfelt, authentic and committed (at least for now).

It may feel tough, but once you have issued your invitation, it is a good time to step back and let things be. By all means ask for an answer by a certain time or date, make clear any wider considerations, and let people know you're looking forward to hearing back from them.

The power of the first mover

In poker, a number of players gather round the table to bet on their cards. The best hand wins – unless everyone else folds their hand first, not being confident that their hand will be worth backing. In each round of betting, there are basically three options for each play – check (not bet, but stay in the hand and await developments), raise (bet more, meaning that anyone else wanting to continue will have to at least match your bet), or fold (throw in your cards and leave the hand, together with any money you've already staked).

Many novice players like to check. After all, it looks like a good bet – you're not putting any more money in; you can see what happens next for free. And maybe everyone will check, so you can get another card for free too, which might improve your hand. A great position – right? Wrong. It's the weakest response. When you check, you hand a great tool of influence to your opponents.

Experienced players have a saying: "Raise or fold." If you think you have a good hand, or think you can bluff your opponents, then raise your bet. By doing this, you'll force all the other players into a position where they are responding to *your* "question" about how good their hands are. The onus is on them for a moment. (The other option, fold, is just to leave the game if you're not wanting to carry on and thus be tempted into chasing a pot with cards that probably aren't good enough.)

Once you've asked your question, let the others have space to think. It's a position with great leadership power – as long as the question is being considered. In real-life leadership, you can't enforce the rules of poker, but you can ensure that everyone has seen your invitation and knows that you are waiting for an answer.

What if people say No?

Remember that in order to get a really authentic Yes, we have to be prepared for the possibility of a No. So, in one way it shows that you made a genuine invitation. At another level, it's a message that your invitation wasn't compelling enough right now, or didn't fit for these people. Maybe they have different ideas about what constitutes a good use of their time?

Take it as a message from the universe. This is easier said than done, but it's much more useful than going around and pleading with them (which rarely works) or bad-mouthing them to your friends.

If you want to carry on engaging those people, start to ask them about what might be more useful, what their priorities are, and when things might be such that they can get involved – all those would be useful possible steps.

Stepping back

As with all the aspects of Host Leadership, the Inviter role involves stepping forward and back, and choosing when to move. Times to step forward and be very positive in inviting include starts, new beginnings, new projects, times when new input and impetus are needed.

Times to step back might be when you've made your point and it's time for someone else. We have found a good saying to be "Don't work harder than everyone else," so if you seem to be making all the running, it may be time to step back and allow others to step forward. Don't keep jumping in – learn to temper your enthusiasm and allow others to catch up and build confidence in their responses. However, if you give too much space, then it can be as if your invitation never existed. As always, it's a balance.

And finally, remember to say *Thank you*! When people accept invitations and are ready to get involved, it is tempting to rush on. A quick word of thanks and acknowledgment will go a long way to cementing relationships and future partnerships.

We will be looking at how to think about *who* to invite (and who not to invite) in the Gatekeeper chapter below.

Inviter

- Think about whom to invite
- What do you need next?
- Offer choice and space for an authentic Yes

- Start with the soft Power of the Ask
- Make it personal, attractive, acknowledging
- Extend a welcoming hand

Reflective questions

- How can you "think invitationally" in the next few days?

- How could you invite participation in an upcoming project or initiative in a way which would engage those you wish to be involved?

- What could you gain from using the Power of the Ask in a surprising way?

- How are you giving choice and space, to allow those around you to step forward with commitment?

- On the rare occasions when you might need to insist… how would you know that the time had arrived and how might you do it?

Key points

> Think invitationally – use soft power in a smart way

> Invitations are acknowledging, attractive – and optional

> Use invitational, not subjugating, language – use questions, be inclusive, use softeners, be positive

> Use the Power of the Ask – even in tough situations

> Give choice and space to get an authentic Yes

8

Space Creator

"Environment is stronger than willpower."

~Buckminster Fuller

 Hosting is intimately connected with space. If we invite people around for a party, it's quite obvious that we then have to put some effort and attention into setting up the space accordingly. Furniture will have to be moved, decorations put up, food and drink prepared, music readied … all to give the party the best chance of being a success.

The space that is created by the host has a powerful influence over what will happen. In particular, the space has to fit what's hoped for and intended. Imagine trying to hold a reception for maximum meeting and interaction in a theater auditorium. Theaters are great spaces for a crammed-in audience watching performers on stage, but they are hopeless for mass interaction and multiple conversations. Whispering to your neighbor or shouting at the person on stage is about the limit of it. Those who work in mass open-plan offices may see a resemblance here.

The space can also include online and cyberspaces. Today, the Web has opened up possibilities for groups and communities to interact around shared interests with little regard for geography. The "space" that is created in the online community is also a key factor – is it supportive or aggressive; are newcomers welcomed or ridiculed; how can different topics be found, engaged with or passed over; how easy is it to find things… These are all part of the space. Setting up and managing the space (or choosing not to manage it) is a key role of a host, and a Host Leader. Much can go wrong when space is mismanaged or not considered carefully.

In this chapter, we will be looking at the role of the Host Leader as a Space Creator. Key topics include:

- The role of space – as a factor in what happens

- Different types of space – physical, interactional, head space

- Making the space fit the place – taking care with details

- Holding the space – stepping back once people have arrived, being aware of how things are going, making adjustments and being prepared to step forward when needed.

The role of space

In starting to think about the role of a host as a Space Creator, a little research reveals many offers of rearranging space, making the most of space, organizing space, de-cluttering, maximizing small spaces, etc. We also hear about such concepts as creating space for you, creating head space, thinking space. There is something deep inside us that knows the importance of space. Good Host Leaders know the importance of space.

The role of host involves creating a suitable space for the events to emerge and unfold. There seems to be a dichotomy here between active planning and emergent responding. Much of the new literature on leadership speaks of the importance of the space and of allowing and nurturing emergence within the space. The host plays a vital role upfront in deciding on the space and how it is to be decorated, laid out and used. This is another example of the flexibility of the host role – one minute making brave and influential decisions and the next clearing up a spilled drink.

The idea of space has been advanced by the idea of *ba*. This Japanese term, originally proposed by philosopher Kitaro Nishida,[1] means "a shared space for emerging relationships" or, in more general terms, a context in which meaning may emerge. Some writers talk of *sacred space* and *safe places* as being of overriding importance. We think that just about any space can be capable of being used with good *ba*. The question, of course, is about how the space is prepared and used, and how the leader's hopes are brought into the space.

Creating space – for things to happen

We would also recognize that different "events" need different spaces: a theater, a restaurant, a political debating chamber, a store, a call center or a factory all clearly have different requirements determined by what we want to achieve in the space. The common denominator of all these different spaces is that they will all contain interactions. Interactions, conversations and relationships will take place in all the "events" or spaces. Returning to the idea of *ba*, space and context are always part of an interaction and give meaning.

Buckminster Fuller, one of the geniuses of the twentieth century, said, "*Environment is stronger than willpower.*" He meant by this that, over and over again, we find that it is easier to succeed in working towards our goals and hopes in environments that support them. Trying to make progress in the face of a space which gets in the way is hard, hard, hard.

When Mark was giving up smoking over twenty years ago, he followed advice from quitting-guru Allen Carr: After having a suitably celebratory last cigarette, clear away all the smoking paraphernalia, wash the ashtrays and get rid of them, remove all lighters, clear away all the evidence that smoking was ever in the house. Then, don't go to the places where you used to smoke regularly, if at all possible, at least until the worst is past. It makes it easier – not easy, but perhaps possible. Mark had a two-week headache and hasn't touched a smoke since.

On a much bigger scale, the gurus of lean manufacturing give great attention to the layout of factories. The idea is usually to minimize movements of work in progress, to have clearly visible signs of what is going on, and to develop a process where work moves along the path in a natural and flowing way to meet customer needs. There is very little room for waste, and where there is waste it becomes visible (and hence can be targeted and reduced). Everything is considered, from the space between machines, to the placing of parts bins, to the visibility of key information for operators. The "right" way to do things also becomes the way of least resistance, the obvious way – and so the space supports the process.

Hosting around the world: The "salon" – space for conversation and connection

Not many people know this now, but one of the early forms of networking has European roots – particularly in France. The *salon* was a form of social gathering popular from the sixteenth century onwards in Europe. A group of people would gather under the roof of a sparkling host (or hostess – *salons* were often convened by women) for a mixture of entertainment and education. Topics would include the arts, literature, poetry and whatever was current, fashionable and interesting at the time.

The *salonnière* (hostess) would have a key role to play, selecting the guests, choosing the topics and mediating the discussion on the day. In an age of male domination, *salons* were a powerful way for women to interact, discuss new ideas and expand their horizons. This kind of gathering continued into the twentieth century. Peggy Guggenheim, New York art collector, art dealer and society hostess, was famed for making her Art of This Century gallery on West 57th Street into a mix of show space and *salon*. Guggenheim was able to connect the new Abstract Expressionist artists such as Jackson Pollock to her wealthy collector friends, and so played a major role in the expansion of modern art. How can *you* connect people from different areas of interest?

Different types of space

As well as physical space, we would like to introduce two other interlinking concepts here – interactional and head space.

Physical space

Physical space is often overlooked in practical leadership writing. We think it's a secret ingredient for success. As well as supporting or interfering with interactions, physical space gives off a whole set of signals and indicators. We will discuss the importance of getting the details right later in the chapter. Having a different physical space can quickly lead to new thoughts, interactions and possibilities. It is no coincidence that people go on retreats or awayday workshops to locations which offer a change of pace and rhythm from everyday work.

Yes to a new future in Ulster

One startling example of this occurred during the Northern Ireland peace agreement negotiations in the late 1990s. David Trimble, later joint winner of the Nobel Peace Prize for ushering in a new era of cooperation to the province, was the leader of the Ulster Unionist Party (UUP), at the time the main Unionist (pro-British) grouping. Ever since the rise of Unionism in the late nineteenth century, the party had rejected calls for agreements which would offer power sharing and cooperation with the (pro-Irish) nationalist parties – a stance characterized by the slogan "Ulster Says No." Trimble knew that he had a fight on his hands to win support from his party faithful for the latest proposal, the Good Friday Agreement, which offered precisely the kind of power sharing the same party had consistently rejected. However, there was an opportunity right on his doorstep for using space creatively.

Previous party meetings had traditionally been held at the Ulster Hall, a Victorian edifice which echoed to the sound of partisan rejection. This time, however, there was a new option. A ceasefire had been in place for the four years previously, which had led to increased confidence in the future and brought major new investments in infrastructure. Part of this was the Waterfront Hall, described by *Time* magazine at the time as a "gleaming modern building that symbolizes the new Ulster."[2] Trimble recognized the opportunity, held the vital mass meeting in the new venue (thereby reminding people of the progress being made in very concrete terms), and his party voted, at last, by fifty-eight percent to forty-two to jettison their core policy and join the new power-sharing executive.

A new space created new interactions – from which emerged a historic shift and a new start for Ulster. Nothing is straightforward in the politics of the province but, although tensions still linger today, this was a true turning point. How might a new space help *you* to some new thinking?

Interactional space

Interactional space is about how it feels to be in a space, and the way we are therefore encouraged to act. How are people treated? How are mishaps responded to? Are people valued or seen as interchangeable cogs in a machine?

A lot has been written about the importance of *safe space*, particularly in the context of difficult conversations. We think this is very useful, and have also been struck by the ways in which some very creative environments deliberately know when to put pressure on people to get high performance. Advertising agencies and fashion designers, for example, seem to thrive on impossible deadlines and last-minute preparation. Indeed, it may be that without the appointment of the pitch or the catwalk show, nothing would get finalized at all. People like to be stretched a little – provided that they have some say in the nature of the stretching.

Likewise, much is made of participation in workplaces. Again, we think this is a very important idea – people should feel able to engage in and contribute to the ways in which their organizations develop. We have also noticed that, occasionally, well-intentioned attempts at involvement founder, when people just want a decision to be made so they can get on with whatever is in store rather than agonizing over it.

This leads us to the idea of the *safe enough* space. If a space is not safe (enough), then people will underperform due to their being nervous, tense and defensive. On the other hand, if a space is too safe (for what is to be done), then the response can be halfhearted, over-relaxed and below par due to the comfortable and predictable nature of the environment. We will look at the benefits of keeping space changing and evolving later in the chapter. The safety – or otherwise – of the space as matters proceed is also a part of the Gatekeeper role – see the next chapter.

Ways to make the space safer include:

- Familiar features – nothing out of the ordinary

- Structure – tables, chairs, barriers, different zones

- A warm welcome – personal connection helps to reassure those arriving

- A clear indication of purpose and roles

Ways to make the space less safe (and perhaps encourage new elements to emerge):

• Unfamiliar elements – perhaps music, lighting, and so on

• Lack of structure – furniture scattered about, perhaps inviting personalization and arrangement

• Abbreviate welcome – just dropping people into the space to see what happens

The creation of a safe enough space is even more challenging in online environments. In forums and discussion groups, it is common to see lists of rules for participation which seem very concerned with what people should not do (don't flame; don't swear; don't query the moderator's decisions…). We prefer guidelines which focus on the interactional – how to be with others – and the positive – what behavior do we wish to see.

A nice example comes from the patient-powered research network PatientsLikeMe. They suggest that ideal PatientsLikeMe members:

• **Ask questions** to help learn about their condition
• **Welcome newcomers** to the community
• **Keep their health profile up to date**, such as disease progress, symptoms, and treatments
• **Share their opinion** with others in a considerate way
• **Respect confidential information** and don't transmit other members' information outside the PatientsLikeMe community
• **Enjoy healthy debate** on the forum but stick to the argument rather than making comments directed at an individual user
• **Check in on other members**, make sure they're okay and help them to keep their profiles accurate and up to date
• **Share personal experiences** without trying to provide medical advice
• **Give feedback** to the PatientsLikeMe Team about potential improvements, questions, or comments about the site

Notice the way these guidelines focus on how to be with other members, rather than on what they should individually do or not do. Safe enough environments do not appear by simply being declared – they need acting and interacting into being.

Head space

Good hosts – and Host Leaders – recognize the need to take time to prepare themselves in advance. They might take time to cast an eye over the final preparations for the event, check that all items have been completed, ensure the stage is set before going off to prepare themselves – get changed, rehearse a speech, mentally rehearse and visualize it going well.

We think of this as "in the kitchen" activity. It is activity that is done out of the limelight and often includes preparation and review. It can also be a recharging time. Without these activities, it is unlikely we will perform at our best; learning won't occur and we can find ourselves repeating the same things over and over yet wondering why.

This type of space is often referred to as *head space*. We might find ourselves needing some quiet time, or thinking time, or time with the door shut, without interruptions. Leaders who routinely make this kind of space for themselves find they create opportunities to step back from the day-to-day and look at the big picture. They plan, review progress and adjust as appropriate. This is time for them to prepare for meetings and conversations, ensuring they maximize the effectiveness of each interaction. Creating head space can allow distance from events that are unfolding, often creating clarity about what to do next for the best outcome.

Techniques such as visualization, mental rehearsal, meditation and mindfulness are all effective practices for finding head space. Once we have experienced the benefits of head space, we become role models for it and advocate it to other members of our teams. Sometimes, when we talk about this concept with clients, their response is that colleagues would wonder what they were doing, almost that it would be frowned upon or laughed at... and most certainly that they don't have time to do it.

However, mental preparation is clearly part of Host Leadership. Imagine the scene if we arrived at an event and the host was still running around organizing things, too busy to welcome us, everything not yet in its place, distracted by many things on their mind, people clearly uncertain about things, asking lots of questions of the host. It wouldn't fill us with confidence about the imminent proceedings or indeed about what the host could deliver in the future.

We have observed over the years that it is not just the host who can benefit from a little head space preparation. Part of the role of a good invitation is to help guests to actively get ready for the event. When they arrive and everything fits together with their expectations, they are then ready to jump in and make wonderful things happen.

Making the space fit the place

"It's important to create spaces that people like to be in, that are humanistic."

~Frank Gehry, architect

When setting up space, details matter. This is something we have found again and again, both in our own experience and in talking to world-class hosts and Host Leaders. Why? Because the details convey many messages, which are read instinctively by those entering the space from outside.

Space conveys many messages

We are constantly forming impressions, and our radar gathers information from many different sources in making those impressions. Like it or not, as people walk into a store, a restaurant, an office or any other space, they are forming impressions of that place. If we walk into a restaurant and notice something about its cleanliness, either good or bad, we form an impression of whether or not we want to eat there, regardless of the fact that we've not seen the kitchen.

In a previous role, Helen advised on the customer service in the branches of a Bank. Among the various aspects of customer service that were measured, two were appearance and efficiency. It was fairly straightforward to observe the appearance of a particular area immediately in view of the customers and to keep it tidy and well stocked with items that would be required; for example, pens and transaction slips. However, it is not always so easy to make the connection between appearance and efficiency unless we put ourselves in the customers' shoes and observe through their eyes. If a pen doesn't work, it inevitably says something about the reliability of the branch overall. Looking beyond the tellers, we might see piles and piles of paper, untidy shelves and rows of disorganized files. How does this make us, as the customer, feel about the service we may be about to get?

On arriving at a business premises, everything, from the car park to the clearly signposted entrance, reception through to the meeting room, conveys a message about that business. We form impressions about the type of organization they are, the reliability, the ease of doing business with them, their attention to detail, the personality of the company. And all from the space: the space conveys the message.

Hosting around the world: Places matter in China

In the West, we are accustomed to dining at rectangular tables, with the host sitting either at the head of the table (the short end, looking down the room at everyone else), or perhaps halfway along one side (the British Prime Minister's traditional seat at the Cabinet table at number 10 Downing Street). This gives prominence to the host. In China, however, it is customary to dine at round tables where there is no "head" position. Instead, the guest is offered the most prominent seat – the one facing the door. The main host will sit next to the guest, usually on his/her left, with the other guests sitting around the table in decreasing order of rank. In domestic settings, it is even customary for the host to sit in the least favored seat, nearest the door and therefore with their back to it. This position also leaves them ready to leap up to welcome new arrivals.

These small things are very culturally specific, and a good Host Leader will take great care in thinking about ways to make their guests feel welcome. Where are *you* sitting? Do you take prominence or do you offer the best places to others?

A context in which meaning can emerge

Host Leaders begin by considering what we want to achieve or what we want to emerge from the interactions of bringing people together. We might want new relationships to emerge, new ideas to surface. We might want to cement existing relationships, show gratitude for them or introduce something new to them. We might want feedback on a new idea – for example, a new product – or to bring people together to help us create a new product. We might be seeking a space where conflict can be acknowledged and trust built. What we are looking to achieve from the event can influence the space we choose. Creating something new might require an informal space with a more informal seating arrangement and flexible refreshment arrangements, whilst launching a new product might be better suited to rows of seats facing a central point, with refreshments in a separate area at prearranged break times.

Different spaces for different faces at Secure IA Ltd.

This connection between space and purpose is well illustrated by the story of Martin Knapp. Martin is the owner-manager of Secure Information Assurance Ltd, a business providing information security services to the UK Government. He and his team took the opportunity of looking at the objectives of different parts of the business and how well suited the space was to helping achieve those objectives.

What they found was that there were two main parts to the business: one being the creative part, designing new releases, solving problems identified by customers; and the other being much more focused on serving existing customers and regular day-to-day work. With this awareness, they looked at the spaces available and designed two completely different workspaces. For the first team, they designed a space with sofas, coffee tables and a water fountain; and for the other team, a more traditional workspace with banks of desks, chairs and computer screens. Both spaces were designed taking into account the meaning that needed to emerge from the space. What's more, the people in the respective teams were best suited to the space designed for their team. This approach has stood the test of time, with a recent refurbishment seeing the continuation of the twin-space solution.

Stepping back and holding the space

"Perhaps one of the most important contributions the language of Host Leadership can make is to move the discourse away from the leader and toward the character and fruitfulness of the space that is created."

Simon Walker, The Leadership Community

As we have seen, preparing space is a key role for a Host Leader, and is one where we can exert quite a lot of choice. This is a chance to step forward, use our skill and judgment and have a considerable influence on what will happen next – when the space is used.

Tending to the space as things go forward is another matter altogether. As a host, we prepare the space knowing that when guests arrive things will get unpredictable – different people may want to do different things, furniture may need to be moved, there will be unexpected events like spillages and so on.

The Host Leader is in the same position. We can't possibly know everything that will happen, and so the space will get changed, messed up and altered. A good Host Leader will be giving a lot of attention to "holding the space."

Advance planning and in-the-moment flexibility

In the Host Leader role of Initiator, we saw that the host initiates something, gets something started. Initiating is also a way to begin to get others invited and involved. If we are going to invite people, it is vital to think about what we are inviting them to and where. This is all about the space. A key part of hosting is making decisions about the space and then creating the space.

The host then has an interesting dilemma – to what extent is he or she the entertainer, the conductor, without whom the conversation dries up? Our experience is that if the host takes on too much of the responsibility for what happens and tries to over-control the space, the potential amongst the guests is limited. Nothing happens without the host – and therefore very little engagement is achieved. It can be exhausting for the host *AND* stifling for the guests.

Now let's transfer this idea to a leadership situation at work. Imagine that a group has been invited to work on a project and the members arrive for the initial meeting. The Host Leader has carefully considered the appropriate space for the initial meeting based on the objectives (hopefully entailing more than just booking a meeting room) and created the space in readiness for the guests arriving. Then what does the good host do as the Space Creator? He/she allows the group to use the space, to rearrange the space as they see fit.

Several years ago, Helen attended an event where the speaker (David Clutter-buck) opened the event, welcomed the audience, who had courteously taken their seats in the neatly laid out rows of chairs, and then invited people to rearrange the space. "This is your space; feel free to move your chairs around and create your learning environment." The impact of this was a highly engaged audience taking responsibility for their own learning. Furthermore, it was memorable! It also highlighted the important effect space can have on allowing things to happen and achieving outcomes. Creating space can include offering people the chance to adapt and modify it, which can be a highly effective tactic.

Holding space for interactions

Hosts can have a very big influence on the space for emergence, and therefore what emerges in the conversations and interactions. Four useful guidelines are:

- Take care to include all voices – both the supportive and the more challeng-ing. It's also useful to consider voices which are being excluded or going unheard.

- Practice curiosity. Being open to new ideas and new learning is vital. If we are not open to it, we will simply miss useful new possibilities.

- Practice respect. All voices and ideas are welcome – but not all ideas have to be accepted.

- Practice generosity, grace and forgiveness. We all make mistakes or say inappropriate things – even the best hosts. It's good to name it, admit it, seek foregiveness and carry on with generosity, instead of blame and criticize space.[3]

When Helen is coaching, one of the ways she describes it is that she is holding a space for the client to do some thinking. It could be said that she is holding a space for meaning to emerge *AND* within which a coaching relationship will emerge. One of Mark's Solutions Focus principles[4] is "The action is in the interaction"; in other words, from that relationship or interaction, action or change will emerge. It is essential that the interaction takes place in a space appropriate for action to emerge.

During coaching, some clients expect to have a coaching conversation in their office, sitting at their desk, in their usual chair and position, invariably with the coach sitting across the desk from them. With all the paraphernalia surrounding the client, the space isn't usually conducive. Instead it is more helpful to arrange a neutral space free from distractions and existing thinking. An interesting alternative is sometimes to go for a walk and coach whilst walking – a very different space, and also a different spatial relationship between us (walking together is a side-by-side activity, whereas sitting is usually face-to-face in some way).

We were having monthly meetings with the senior management team of an IT support company. These were taking place in the restaurant of a local hotel around a superb round table tucked away in the corner. It was a regular favorite spot of the managing director. There was no doubt about its privacy, facilities, away from day-to-day work distractions. However, as the team grew to three plus the facilitator, the noise levels began to interfere, and we needed the flexibility to use a flipchart as and when appropriate. As the relationships developed and the interactions changed, we identified the need to switch the space and moved to a new venue, with great extra results.

What is key is being constantly aware of the changing needs and questioning the appropriateness of the space, to ensure it is still working.

Renewal and adjustment

A lot of effort can go into making sure that the space continues to be a great platform for what's happening. At one level, this means taking care that the space is renewed from time to time – freshened up, put back, even repaired. A Host Leader will be in a stepped-back position for some of the time, and is therefore in a great position to notice what is out of place, and deal with it quickly.

Attention to detail at Le Manoir

Professional hosts set great store by taking care of their spaces. Philip Newman-Hall, director at Raymond Blanc's legendary Oxfordshire restaurant Le Manoir aux Quat'Saisons, says that it's all in the detail:

> *"The big picture just happens if you look after the small things. Guests know that very occasionally big things will go wrong – a power cut to the boiler so no hot water in the rooms. They understand that. But if there is a small thing out of place, they notice and then start looking for other small things. There is a light bulb gone in their room. A name is wrong on a place card. They are wished happy birthday, not happy anniversary. And these things matter."*[5]

Philip really walks his talk, too. When Mark visited him, Philip noticed some rust on a garden chair. Before the interview ended an hour later, the rust was already being attacked to reduce it immediately, prior to the chair being replaced as soon as possible.

This is a very key idea – the detail may be more important, in some ways, than the big picture. As a Host Leader, we will sometimes have to use some pretty unsuitable spaces. The question is not then to moan about this particular office block or location, but to do everything we can to get the details right, so that it's the best it can be for the staff and visitors to interact productively. The search for a better office block can then go on separately over a longer timescale.

Top British hotelier Harry Murray is equally clear about the leader's role in maintaining the space – even at a very menial level. He says:

> *"I expect everyone to take an active role – including myself. I will pick up rubbish. I'll ask, 'Can I have a broom?' if there is rubbish, rather than ask someone else to clean it up. (They will usually then leap to clean it up anyway…)."*[6]

We find time and again that leaders who can (some of the time) focus on the small details will be seen in a new and useful light by their people. Being aware of the power of detail shows caring more than any grand gesture does. Both authors have been frustrated at attending conferences which say that the world needs changing, but at which the organizers show themselves to be incapable of providing coffee or fresh air, let alone changing environmental policy.

Noticing and supporting what is emerging

As time goes on, the Host Leader will, from a stepped-back position, be very aware of noticing what is actually happening and emerging. Of course, one way to do this is simply to compare it with our hopes and intentions, and to take action to nudge things in that direction when the time is right.

However, there is a more challenging possibility. Sometimes, what is emerging is not what we had hoped for – it's even better! Unexpected happenings can be very useful indeed – providing they are not shut down by a leader who is too keen to stick to his/her plans and is not noticing the possibility of what is happening before his/her eyes.

Mark was recently helping to host a workshop with the digital team from a leading London museum. The agenda, agreed and discussed in advance, was about honing a new digital strategy. As the team gathered and said hello, however, it was clear that other events were at the top of their minds: the arrival of a new chief executive from outside, combined with messages arriving about further budget cuts, were getting in the way of views of the long-term strategy. The group agreed that the new events needed considering, and so the focus of the workshop shifted to examining the opportunities presented by the changes and how the digital team could present themselves as a vital and potent resource in the short term.

World Leadership Day Singapore organizer Denise Wright puts this awareness very nicely:

> *"Holding the space can be hero-like – with the leader as a 'key holder' who controls what happens, or more host-like where the host gently steers the group to hold the space collectively. The Host Leader is still actively steering and participating but in a gentle, easygoing, almost invisible way. This host-like holding the space is dedicated to connection and to development, to people being their own experts, to possibility, potential, and graceful shared progress and evolution."*[7]

Changing the space in a big way

Sometimes we need to consider changing our spaces in a big way. This can be a forced move – that the lease on the building is up, or even that the area is scheduled for demolition. It can also be a powerful choice, however, for a leader wanting to change their organization. There is now a great interest in how workplaces can be designed and maintained not simply as a place for everyone to go, but as a key part of an organization's success.

As global head of group property at mining group Rio Tinto, Neil Usher was responsible for moving the London offices from a traditional building in the financial district to a newly constructed modern block near Paddington station. The old building was traditional in design, with lots of individual offices, name plates on doors and so on. The new office gave Neil the chance to be creative and think widely about how the building could support the kinds of collaboration the organization was seeking. Neil told us:

> *"You can't be afraid of experimenting. Planning is overrated. However much you plan, and however much effort you put into asking people what they want, some things will not work out as you hoped. This sends us in the direction of flexibility – using furniture to build the space, rather than walls and concrete. However, physical openness doesn't create collaboration – you need to make places where people will talk to each other. And we spend about half our time in focused quiet work, so people need spaces to do that as well."*

Neil is also clear about the importance of detail. Rio Tinto's office features a large café right by the front door, outside the turnstiles and security system, where people can meet visitors and work together at street level.

> *"It's about connecting to life outside the building. The café is very well-used – which meant that the coffee areas we had carefully planned within the building are less used than had been hoped for. The urban, public metaphor is extremely important in this regard - and its proximity to the street helped significantly. It really feels like you are in a high street environment, not an office. We had people come in off the street and ask if it was okay to use it."*[8]

We can't go into the many aspects of workplace design here. What we are stressing is that creating and re-invigorating an effective workplace is a vital leadership task. Neil's findings fit very well with the Initiator role of the Host Leader – having a long-term direction in mind, then taking small steps, seeing what happens, and adjusting. Being prepared to adjust as we go along does not mean we were wrong to start with; it's a flexible and pragmatic response to the inevitable uncertainties of the modern world of work.

Stepping back

Having created our space, we will then be moving on to inviting people (Inviter), welcoming them over the threshold (Gatekeeper) and connecting with them (Connector). All this means stepping back from the role of Space Creator, trusting that our preparations have been effective.

We will then be watching from our stepped-back position to see how people are using the space, how it might be adjusted, renewed and altered. And then we can step forward again in the Space Creator role.

Space Creator

- What would be a great space – physical, interactional and head space
- What message is your space conveying?
- Hold the space while people use it

- Create a space to support what you want to happen
- Focus on the details as well as the big picture
- Keep the space refreshed, invigorated and evolving

Reflective questions

- What messages is your space conveying – to your people, to customers, to visitors? How could it convey more useful messages?

- Which area would be most useful for you to focus on first – physical space, interactional space or head space? (By paying attention to one, the others will change too.)

- How are you taking action to renew and invigorate the space – starting with small details?

- When might you want to make some big changes to your space, to shake things up and produce a next-generation space for your people?

Key points

➤ Step forward proactively to create a useful space.

➤ Step back to hold the space, adjust it, reinvigorate it or even change it completely.

➤ There are many possibilities with space – don't take it for granted.

➤ Space reflects culture, expectations, what an organization does.

➤ Attention to detail is vital – the details make all the difference.

9

Gatekeeper

"Hospitality is about the crossing of thresholds, the re-imagining of boundaries and the negotiation of space."

~Mary David Walgenbach OSB,
Sisters of Saint Benedict of Madison, Wisconsin

 Gatekeeping is one of the roles most associated with hosts around the world. Who else if not a host can invite you over their threshold into their space, to the discovery and creation of new possibilities? And who else if not a host can, under certain circumstances, ask you to leave?

In this chapter, we will look at the many possibilities in the Gatekeeper role for Host Leaders to creatively and rapidly impact the performance of our organizations. It's easy to think of a Gatekeeper as someone who mostly excludes people from entering, like a bouncer outside a nightclub. While this can occasionally be a valuable intervention, the Gatekeeper is more often concerned with drawing boundaries that will help create and sustain progress. These may be in terms of people involved, in terms of rules and routines, and in terms of psychological safety. As we will see, there are links here to the Space Creator role.

In hosting terms, the host as gatekeeper is often actually standing by the "gate" – the door. They decide who gets to enter the space, and on what terms. Imagine a situation where you have invited six carefully chosen friends around to your house for a long-planned celebration meal. On the night, one of the guests arrives with their new partner – who they only just met and neglected to tell you about. It's a difficult situation – do you allow them in or not? This is very poor behavior on the part of the guest, of course – they should have called ahead to check the situation. As hosts, we have ways to deal with this kind of situation – turning both away would severely damage your relationship, so most hosts would let them in and somehow make it work.

In the public arena, we have already mentioned the connection with bouncers, outside a nightclub. While these gatekeepers have had a poor reputation in some places, their role is in fact to keep everyone safe, defuse tension and build communication, rather than resort to physical violence. The profession is using training and licensing to build a more constructive role and image.

Hosts also look after the gate from the other side. When the evening is done, the host may finally invite everyone to leave. They may need to exclude or even throw out misbehaving guests. The choices around this – to let in, to turn away, to throw out – are always the host's responsibility.

In Host Leadership terms, these choices are even more varied and important. As we will see in this chapter, the Host Leader is not simply welcoming or excluding people – we make choices all the time about what to allow, what to encourage, what to exclude in terms of topics, questions, people and responsibilities. The Host Leader will wish to establish and maintain integrity in the group or organization. They may well be hosting different subgroups within the overall organization – project teams, committees with certain responsibilities, different contexts which will have different norms. These all feature different gates to keep, norms to be established and decisions to be made.

In this chapter, we will examine how you can host well using these ideas:

- Boundaries and thresholds – insiders and outsiders

- Container size – choosing the boundaries

- Boundary-spanning leadership

- Closing the gate

Boundaries and thresholds – insiders and outsiders

"Hospitality begins at the gate, in the doorway, on the bridges between public and private space. Finding and creating threshold places is important for contemporary expressions of hospitality."

~Christine D Pohl[1]

A Host Leader knows the importance (and the creative possibilities) of defining boundaries. In the postmodern world of the Internet, boundaries have had a bad press – some say that there are no boundaries anymore. On the contrary; a boundary can serve the Host Leader well by making clear what expectations and norms apply. In the same way as a host can have a "leave your shoes in the hall and don't tramp mud into my carpet if you're in this house" norm, the Host Leader will take care to choose boundaries that can help people understand where they are and what they are committing to do in a certain place or role.

Once people have come over the threshold, they are aware of being in a new place, with new people and possibly new expectations. One of the key roles of a Host Leader is to welcome newcomers as they cross the threshold – this also gives an excellent chance to share something of the routines and rituals of the organization. Alert readers will remember the story of the Benedictines and greeting everyone as the risen Christ from Chapter 2.

We have heard in Chapter 8 about Mark's visit to the famous Manoir Aux Quat'Saisons restaurant and hotel in Oxfordshire, UK. The Manoir, under founder and Chef Raymond Blanc, is noted for high standards of hospitality, and Mark had arranged to meet Director/General Manager Philip Newman-Hall to discover how these standards were achieved. Mark arrived a moment or two after the expected ten a.m., and was amazed and delighted to find Philip waiting for him outside the front door! What a contrast to going to most companies, where the manager is hidden in an office as far from the front door as possible and surrounded by defensive lines of secretaries. We sometimes wonder how it might be if the manager were positioned by the door, so he/she could connect with those going in and out – it could be a hugely valuable position to adopt.

Hosting around the world: The tale of the wet doorstep

In Japan, it is customary for specially invited visitors to a temple complex to arrive and discover that the main doorstep is wet. This indicates that the step has just been cleaned, which is a sign of respect to the guests, and an indicator that they are expected. The wet step is a sign both of the importance of the guests, the readiness of the host and the start of an excellent interaction. How could you welcome visitors in an imaginative and appropriate way?

Routines, rituals and expectations

There are all kinds of rituals and routines which help give coherence – these can range from the very simple (an operational meeting for the management team every day at nine a.m. to set priorities) to the bizarre (all new members must survive a ritual rolling in a filthy barrel – the traditional initiation for newly qualified whisky-barrel makers, or coopers, at the Speyside Cooperage in Scotland). Some make excellent operational sense; some act as defining the organization; some are rooted in history; some show a purpose in reminding people of why things are how they are.

During the State opening of parliament in the UK, for example, the Queen arrives in the House of Lords and then sends her representative, the heraldically-titled Black Rod, to fetch the elected members from the House of Commons. Black Rod then walks to the door of the Commons only for it to be slammed (ritually) in his face. This gesture symbolizes the independence of the elected parliament from the sovereign. He then knocks three times on the door, and is finally admitted. This piece of pantomime is all part of remembering how things have come to be, a far cry from the days before democracy.

It is for the Host Leader to establish and lead these routines – or to change them if they have served their purpose and their time has passed. It is a very strong leadership move to change a tradition – a clear sign of a new way of doing things. To continue with traditions, on the other hand, is a sign of continuity. Perhaps the ultimate such sign is the portrait of Chairman Mao Zedong which hangs over Tiananmen Square in Beijing – it shows that this is still the same People's Republic of China that Mao led, whatever capitalist and modern ways are being adopted.

Routines and safety

One powerful purpose of routines is that they help all involved feel somehow safe – that things are still going on as they have gone on before, and that we are still all part of the same institution. In this context, the role of the Host Leader is an example of what Professor Ralph Stacey calls, "A good enough holding of anxiety."[2] There is a lot of talk about the need for people to feel "safe" to perform well, and it's time to look at this aspect of leadership here.

If people feel totally safe, they may in time feel little incentive to perform or innovate. If people feel very anxious, they will put all their energy into self-preservation and will similarly not give of their best. So, somewhere between these is a zone where performance is at its maximum. This is often called something like "safety." However, people are much more likely, in real and changing organizational settings, to be anxious. The task of the Host Leader, therefore, can be to mitigate this anxiety to some extent, with "holding" it being preferable to totally eliminating it – as we already discussed in the Space Creator role.

Helen was working with managers from all disciplines within airline MyTravel as part of their annual management development program. This particular year the program coincided with the announcement that MyTravel was to merge with Thomas Cook. This caused much anxiety, not just amongst the managers, but also amongst their teams. At times of great change, people's natural desire is for more communication – and often what they get is less. However, the Managing Director of MyTravel scheduled a weekly conference call for all managers to dial into. This was an opportunity for weekly updates direct from the MD. What's more, if there was nothing to report, the call still went ahead, so that communication was maintained. This is a great example of holding the anxiety and helping people to feel "safe" during uncertain times.

Beginnings and endings are good times to set up routines and rituals. Even a simple process of starting a certain meeting by asking everyone what they are most pleased with at work at the moment can both produce valuable sharing of information, lift the energy of the room (people enjoy talking about their successes, and they sometimes get little enough chance), and announce that we are here again and that things are running as they "should." Perhaps there are enough surprises in the world already, so we don't need any more than really necessary in the workplace?

It is of course possible that the Host Leader may need to inject a little uncertainty from time to time if everything is getting too cozy. Innovating and experimenting with new routines and rituals is a very good way for the Host Leader to jiggle things up a bit, to set up a new framework and to keep everyone on their toes. What is a good level of routine for *your* organization?

Insiders and outsiders

If there are to be "insiders" within a particular gate, there must also, by definition, be "outsiders." This happens all the time in organizations – another department, the "Swindon lot" from the Office in the next town; those who are invited to the chairman's garden party; the new recruits; the new foreign owners; the people from headquarters who come to "help," and so on. Many groups throughout history have taken their identity, and even their name, from those labeling them as "outsiders." The Yankees (inhabitants of the northeastern states of the USA from the eighteenth century) were so called by those out to belittle them, notably the English in the War of Independence and the Southern Confederate states of the Civil War. In more modern times, we have seen the word "queer," originally an insult to homosexuals, taken and used assertively by the gay community.

One role of a Host Leader is to deal with and welcome outsiders. Even though they may be from elsewhere, they are still to be valued and made welcome in the appropriate places. Seth Godin in his book *Tribes*[3] on the other hand, encourages us to positively exclude outsiders as part of the definition of who "we" are. While there may be power in the definition gained by excluding, there is also some pain, and it is up to the Host Leader to figure out the balance of usefulness.

We sometimes find that we have accidentally excluded people who should have been invited. Sometimes they are from within the organization, but we find that more often the overlooked include subcontractors, suppliers and other externals. In this case, taking particular care to greet and welcome them will pay dividends. Make clear that there was a mix-up, pay special attention and help the formerly excluded people really feel like insiders.

Next, let us look at a crucial but often overlooked element in the leadership equation – the benefits of larger or smaller "container size."

Flexing the container – choosing the boundaries

We usually think of a container as a jar or box of some kind – something in which to hold other things. The idea of a "container " in organizational terms comes from Ed Olson and Glenda Eoyang.[4] Olson and Eoyang are familiar with viewing the world as a place of emergence and complexity. This is the kind of place where Host Leadership can thrive. Their slightly abstract idea of a container in organizational terms is a context with boundaries.

We can start thinking about containers as groups of people in organizational life – this team, that department, this project group. This is one factor, but it's not the end of the story. The container may also have elements of the physical (a certain room or place), behavioral (professional identities such as doctors, lawyers or IT people), cultural identities (such as new starters or Australians), and conceptual (what is discussed here, what is open and what is not). We can view these factors as levers the Gatekeeper uses to flex or manage the container to achieve a desired outcome. Using the levers, the Gatekeeper might consider: who to involve, where something might take place, what behaviors are required, and how things will operate, what cultural identities might exist or be adopted and what will be discussed or what is the question to be addressed.

We will be members of many different containers at work – different groups, different settings. The board meeting is a classic container – a certain group, usually meeting in a certain place, with certain responsibilities and norms. Later, when the board meets on a strategy awayday, the container will be different (in terms of place and the questions to be discussed, as well as dress codes and other expectations). And when some of the board members go off to meet potential customers or present at an industry conference, those too are different containers.

As a host, it is vital that we think carefully about the containers we are working in: too big or weak and things will get unmanageable; too small or strong and staleness will creep in. We are looking for something in between – just right. Adjusting the container is a key part of the Gatekeeper role.

Container size and strength

One good way to start thinking practically about containers is in terms of size and strength.

Size is usually related to the number of people involved. It also connects to the range of views and positions to be found within the group. A few people with a clear focus and agreed goals might be seen as a 'small' container. If there is major divergence about key issues, then the container is bigger. A large gathering of people from diverse backgrounds would be a relatively large container – requiring different approaches to host than the small team, but with the possibility of more creative and innovative outcomes.

Strength, on the other hand, is nothing to do with size. It is about the coherence and alignment of the container – the sharpness of definition, the things that draw people together and the norms they follow in the space. A strong container will have well-defined boundaries and expectations; a weak one will be much more fuzzy. Of course, there are many elements involved here, not all of which may be clearly weak or strong. For example, a small management team meeting every week with a clearly defined agenda would probably be a strong container, whereas the same number of random people sitting coincidentally in a railway waiting room would be a very weak container (probably requiring a major disaster just outside the door to motivate them into collective action). Of course at times a weak, fuzzy container may be ideal. The Host Leader as Gatekeeper then brings more shape or clarity as required by adjusting the size and strength levers of the container.

We can think of some everyday examples of containers and how they work. Parliamentary systems, for example, involve many members (large size) and so adopt some strict rules and protocols (strong strength) in order to work effectively. Small entrepreneurial businesses, on the other hand, may be very small with a handful of committed individuals (small size), who will therefore be able to act coherently with a much more wide-ranging, flexible and ad hoc set of processes (weaker strength).

Choosing and changing container size

The Host Leader will learn to have a keen eye on the containers of which they are a part, and in particular those that they host. There is a strong general rule here: if something is getting difficult to manage and not producing results, make the container smaller or stronger. If things need an injection of new thinking, make the container bigger or weaker.

The table below shows how different basic containers offer different starting points.

Size	**Large, weak ("diverse community")** Upside: Very diverse, many views, many possibilities Downside: hard to manage, difficult to get things done	**Large, strong ("movement")** Upside: Can become a loud and clear voice, focusing attention and action Downside: Can become exclusive, risk of fragmentation, only see limited possibilities
	Small, weak ("group of acquaintances") Upside: Intimate and wide-ranging discussions can lead to innovation, close relationships can develop more easily Downside: May need nurturing and keeping going, without a strong central focus	**Small, strong ("focused team")** Upside: Very strong focus for developing ideas and action Downside: May become rigid, lacking flexibility, over-predictable, isolated from reality

Strength

Increasing or decreasing the size and strength of the container is a key way to respond to a developing situation. Here are some things to think about:

Increasing size: Will bring in more voices and differences. Advantage: Wider discussion and input, wider commitment to the results (if handled well). Drawback: May become hard to manage and keep track of if not handled well.

Decreasing size: Reducing the numbers involved, and perhaps the variance of views. Advantage: Easier to have a participative and engaging interaction. Drawback: May miss key aspects of a discussion.

Increasing strength: Making the 'question' or process more focused and tight. Advantage: Helps to focus contributions and inputs, and provides a better clue as to when enough has been done. Drawback: If the wrong question is considered, opportunities are missed, people with different concerns may feel excluded.

Decreasing strength: Broadening the 'question' or process. Advantage: A wider scope may allow many different aspects to be considered. Drawback: May not produce direct actions or progress, should these be required.

These levers can be used together to help make difficult discussions more manageable. For example, setting up a small task force to address a specific issue is to make a container which is smaller and stronger. Having a wide consultation about the future of our organization is to make a large and less strong container (possibly for good reason).

A Host Leader is aware of the times when employing these levers can help to build progress in challenging times. It's not as simple as strong is good, weak is bad and so on – the container should be adjusted to match the context.

	Decrease Strength	Increase Strength
Increase Size	**Increase size, decrease strength** Draw in more people around a more general topic. Good for strategic reviews and widescale reflection.	**Increase size and strength:** Bring in more people to consider a well-focused question. Good for generating commitment and buy-in.
Decrease Size	**Decrease size and strength** A smaller number of people addressing more general topics. Good for building relations and exploring possibilities – 'the team that drinks together thinks together'.	**Decrease size, increase strength** A smaller number of people addressing a well-focused question. Good for producing action steps and concrete proposals.

Sometimes, the Host Leader will be seeking to expand the container – to involve more people, to get new ideas, to generate new possibilities – by asking "*What's missing here?*" On other occasions when there are difficult decisions to be made, it may be better to shrink the container, either by involving fewer people, or by focusing attention. On this occasion, "*What can be left out?*" might be a better question. It's not surprising that events involving a whole nation – such as referendums – are boiled down into a (usually) simple yes/no question – this is a large number, but a strong structure. The smaller and stronger the container, the more focused (and constrained) it can be. The larger and weaker the container, the more wide-ranging and diverse (and unconstrained) it can be.

A large yet strong container: Chris Anderson and TED

TED started life in 1984 as a conference for new development in technology, entertainment and design. British computer magazine entrepreneur Chris Anderson took over the annual TED conference in 2001, and has shown himself to be an excellent Host Leader by the way he has increased the reach and influence of the organization by creating a very strong container – strong enough to withstand expanding in size in many ways.

The focus of the annual TED conference since 1990 has been the eighteen-minute talk – "Long enough to be serious, and short enough to hold people's attention," says Anderson. This duration is very strictly observed during TED events – a large clock is displayed to the presenters, and anyone overrunning is basically gonged off. This in turn brings clarity and focus – what is the idea to be communicated? Also, none of the presenters had an off-the-shelf eighteen-minute talk available, so they had to refine their material. TED events also have very strong guidelines about what is and is not allowed in terms of branding, attendees, no selling, organisation, and many other factors. This creates a very strong container in which a rich mixture of topics can work together. Without the strong format, we suggest, TED would never have attained such dramatic growth in reach and popularity.

Until 2006, the annual TED conferences were basically invitation-only high ticket price events, with the invites highly prized. Anderson then oversaw a huge expansion in the reach of TED – first by starting to post videos of the talks online for free (and it turns out that eighteen minutes works well online), opening up the conferences to public application, starting a TED Fellows program for brilliant young scientists, artists and activists, and expanding the range of conferences to reach other parts of the world. Then, most audaciously,

Anderson decided to open the organizing of TED conferences with the TEDx program – anyone could apply to host a TED-like event, using the TED branding, and offer the videos for online posting. At the time of writing, there are several thousand TEDx events every year – and all this achieved with a staff of just ninety people.

In our view, Anderson has created and nurtured such a strong container in the TED Talks that he has been able to invite a vast number into his (carefully nurtured) space. He is also very active in the space – at conferences, Mark (who has coached TED Fellows as part of the SupporTED scheme) has found him to be visible, involved, engaged and active, running sessions and being available for conversation.

Building a workable container: Developing governance at the Sunday Assembly

Mark was facing a tough challenge in developing a governance process for the Sunday Assembly movement. With some thirty chapters started on a wave of enthusiasm, some sort of structure would be required to allow everyone a say on future developments, in a way that would not hinder the flexibility needed by a new and emerging network.

This is a classic example of a difficult container. It's quite a large one in terms of people involved – there were upwards of two hundred members on the Internet discussion group, which formed the main channel for group communication. It's also a big question – how to organize a new global grouping of a novel type which has never been seen before, run by free-thinkers. To make the situation more manageable, Mark had three basic options – make the size smaller, increase the strength by focusing the discussion, or both.

Reducing size: Mark asked the whole network for their hopes and priorities for a new governance system. Around ten people replied. As well as giving useful ideas, these people had just become an initial smaller group for discussion of the issue – they had already shown themselves willing.

Making the container stronger: Mark then worked up some detailed proposals based on the initial ideas and his own research into similar organizations. This proposal was quietly circulated around some of the small group, for comment and development. What was once a very large question had now become a much more focused one – "*What do you think of this?*"

As the proposals became more refined and stronger, Mark was able to include more and more people in the discussion (increasing the size) without risking the whole thing losing shape. There were some strong debates and differences of view – but at least around something that was well formed and could be clearly referenced. A final proposal was discussed by the whole community and amended before being voted in with overwhelming support.

When we are seeking to grow organisations – whether businesses or communities – it's tempting to focus only on the number of people involved. However, there is a growing view that it's the quality and richness of interactions, rather than the number of people, that lead to sustainable growth.

Growing by numbers or by interactions

Seth Godin in his book *Tribes* talks about three ways that leaders can seek to grow and enhance the impact of the "tribes" – groups of people with a shared interest – they lead:

1. Transforming the shared interest into a passionate goal and desire for change (i.e., increasing strength)

2. Providing tools to allow other members to tighten their communications (again, increasing strength)

3. Leveraging the tribe to allow it to grow and gain new members (increasing size)

Godin says most leaders focus on the third tactic. The other two "almost always lead to more impact." Here he is talking about strengthening the container, rather than increasing the number of people. A good Gatekeeper will have an eye on the coherence of the container – and the benefits from varying it. Simply growing the size may not have the most impact in the long term – indeed, if the wrong people start arriving, the result could be either disastrous or (possibly) transformational. It's all part of the uncertainty of the emerging world.

This thinking is echoed by online communities guru Richard Millington, author of *Buzzing Communities*. He says that the number of members of an online community tells us almost nothing about how strong the community is. What makes a strong and viable community is the richness of interactions *between* the members. These can take many forms, including conveying information, bonding and status-jockeying.[5] However, it's the *interaction* that makes the community – not the *individuals*. This is the nub of the container in the Gatekeeper role – flexing the container to ensure the quality of the interaction to achieve the desired purpose/outcome.

Boundary-spanning leadership

Having created and sustained some good working containers, the Host Leader will also be on the lookout for opportunities for "boundary spanning." This term comes from research from the Center for Creative Leadership.[6] Questioning senior executives, they identified boundary spanning as one competence which was regarded as very important but not done very well or very often. Boundary spanning is, naturally, about working across boundaries – vertical, horizontal, stakeholder, demographic, and geographic – to create results not achievable within one set of boundaries.

We have learned already about the importance of welcoming outsiders when they show up. The other side of the equation is that the Host Leader will be going off to cross other boundaries, discover new ideas and build new relationships. This means knowing how to be a good guest as well as a good host. Knowing how and when to welcome outsiders, and being adroit at joining in with other communities, Host Leaders will be very well equipped to boundary span by connecting, respecting others' spaces and co-participating.

Hosting around the world: Respecting boundaries in the Torres Straits Islands

The natives of the Torres Straits Islands (between Papua New Guinea and Australia) have strict customs about crossing boundaries. Kanat Wano, a Meriam man from Mer (Murray Island) in the Zenadh Nation told us that "walking on someone else's country" was a serious matter. Respecting the land is very important. "You might stand there for three days on a boundary, waiting and calling," he told us. The protocol is that you can't go onto someone else's land unless you get permission. The respect you show for the boundary and the land translates into safe passage and assistance.

A Host Leader will not barge in uninvited. We can make clear our interest and desire to visit, and then approach the boundary and show respect. Judging when it's okay to make gestures of friendship and connection is another aspect of boundary spanning. This aspect is shown brilliantly by one of our exemplar Host Leaders – Nelson Mandela.

Spanning two warring cultures with a shirt – Nelson Mandela

You may be familiar with the iconic scene of Nelson Mandela presenting the Rugby World Cup to SA captain Francois Pienaar on the afternoon of June 24th, 1995 – wearing the Springbok jersey with Pienaar's number six on the back. The story was dramatized in the movie *Invictus*, with Morgan Freeman and Matt Damon. It was an image of gate-opening and reconciliation which went a very long way to connect black and white South Africans. This was but one moment in a very long journey of gate-opening and connecting by Mandela.

Mandela was sentenced to life imprisonment in 1964. Forced into hard labor, he nonetheless took a lot of trouble to engage as much as possible with his jailers, learning Afrikaans in the process. He became well aware of the huge importance of rugby to white Afrikaner South Africans – the blacks were much more interested in soccer. Then his colleagues wanted to get rid of the iconic Springbok name for the rugby team. Again, Mandela worked them around to keeping it. "They" were now "Us."

Mandela went to visit the team himself – at their training ground. He was well received, and three-quarter back Hennie le Roux offered Mandela his Springbok cap as a thank you. Mandela was delighted, and wore the cap there and then. He wore the cap to the opening ceremony of the World Cup – where SA beat Australia 27-18. He also wore the cap to an ANC rally, where his party gave him a hard time about it, but again he won them around. The tournament progressed and South Africa reached the final.

The idea of wearing the jersey came from Mandela's security guard, Linga Moonsamy, on the day of the final. The whole security team thought it a grand idea and presented it to Mandela, who instantly saw the potency of such a gesture and added the idea that it should be Pienaar's number six. The only trouble was – they didn't have one! A number six jersey and another cap were rapidly procured (Mandela having left le Roux's cap at his residence in Cape Town). South Africa won the dramatic final 15-12, with Joel Stransky scoring a drop goal in extra time to clinch the victory, and Mandela walked out to present the Webb Ellis cup to Pienaar with both men sporting the same jersey. The whole of South Africa – black as well as white – rejoiced.[7]

Crossing the boundary in solitary confinement: the amazing tale of Sidney Rittenberg

Sidney Rittenberg was one of the very few American citizens to be close to the Chinese communist regime during the rise to power of Mao Zedong. Studying Chinese in the US Army, he was sent to China in 1944, decided to stay on after the end of World War II and met the leadership of the Communist party in 1946. On occasion he was asked by Mao and other top officials to translate messages and documents.

Mao's Communists won power in 1949; Mao was appointed Chairman of the People's Republic of China, and Rittenberg was put into solitary confinement for supposed involvement in a Russian spy network. He spent the first year without seeing his captors – they passed him food though a slot and observed him through a peephole. He survived this time by remembering a poem from his childhood by Edwin Markham:

> *"He drew a circle that shut me out –*
> *Heretic, a rebel, a thing to flout.*
> *But Love and I had the wit to win:*
> *We drew a circle that took him in."*

Rittenberg decided that the only way to reach out was to create a powerful experience of love for his captors. When they looked through the peephole, he emitted in every way he could that he was encircling them. He took his toothbrush and cleaned his cell as high up on the walls as he could; he demonstrated his compassion for his captors by meditating every day. After a while, the guards began to provide books and a candle by which to read. He didn't ask for anything; he expressed appreciation, love and respect for the Chinese people. By drawing the boundary to include his unseen captors, he created an environment for survival. After five years of imprisonment, reha-bilitation and a further nine years in jail during the Cultural Revolution, Rittenberg finally left China in 1979, returned to the USA and established a successful consultancy, helping corporations in their dealings with the East.[8]

Closing the gate

So far, this chapter has mostly been about making use of gate-opening methods to build a great working container for results – the right people, the right questions, the right routines, the right level of holding anxiety, the right level of boundary spanning, and new horizons. However, sometimes it is the role of the Gatekeeper to bar the way, to close the gate and to exclude people or questions.

This can be seen as a very negative position. After all, wouldn't we all like to be welcoming people in all the time? Sometimes, however, a Host Leader will decide that the container has got too large, in terms of the number of people, or too weak, in terms of the focus. Then it may be time to close the gate on somebody or something.

This is never an easy time, and it's a last resort to cast someone out into the wilderness. There may be ways to adjust the container size without actually throwing people out from the whole event.

Make a new container

Find a new place to convene a smaller and more focused group to work on a particular topic. This can then be fed into the larger group at an appropriate time. For example, suppose there is dissatisfaction at a particular policy; rather than discussing it with everyone and risking unnecessary friction and uncertainty, a smart Host Leader may decide to form a working group to look at the situation and report back.

Make a temporary change

Introduce a new and more focused container for an experimental period. During particularly busy periods, some organizations change their rules and norms so that it's all hands to the pumps. Supermarket giant Tesco has been known to cope with the huge rush at Christmas by sending nearly five thousand head-office staff – including buyers, HR staff and directors – to work in over a thousand stores in the run-up to the holiday period.[9] This has the advantage that everyone knows it's temporary, and that normal service will be resumed. It is not impossible that interesting new practices and more permanent shifts may be discovered from such experiments. We heard of a new head teacher who wanted to do away with the end-of-lesson bell in his school. The staff rebelled, saying they couldn't possibly do without it. In the end, the head told the staff that it was broken! (They quickly learned to do without it and never went back.)

Give a positive No

If not allowing someone through the gate, or even excluding them, is necessary, then the Host Leader will ensure that this is done in the most constructive fashion possible. William Ury's outstanding work on the power of a positive No[10] gives some excellent pointers for this. Ury incisively points out the tension between the leader exerting their power on the one hand, and needing to tend to their relationship with the excluded person on the other. If (as in the nightclub bouncer situation) you have absolutely no need for any continuing relationship, then feel free to exclude away! However, in real-life leadership situations, there is almost always a need to preserve and even build relationships for what may come next.

A positive No therefore maintains and builds relationship as well as getting the immediate need dealt with. It basically takes the form "Yes! No. Yes?"

1. **Yes!** Acknowledge the interest, contribution, enthusiasm or whatever else the person has shown. Be specific if you can – let them know you have noticed the positive and useful elements of the situation so far.

2. **No.** State what you need to have happen clearly and as a matter of fact. Giving a justifiable reason for your position can help here – it shows that this is perhaps not the situation you were hoping for, and that you have not taken your decision lightly.

3. **Yes?** Offer an alternative action, role or possibility to the other person. This will both achieve your goal and also offer another way for the relationship with the person to continue. This may be another way to be involved with the project, another contribution that they might make, a point in the future where this can be revisited, another route for the person to take.

This third phase offers something for people to agree with, and so be able to maintain and even build relationships. So this No is not the end of everything, but a point of punctuation along the road of a continuing and valued partnership.

Let's look at an example. Laura is Gillian's manager. Gillian can act as a host, even when she isn't one, with a positive No.

Laura: I'm looking for someone talented to chair our ethics committee. It's a sensitive position, with lots of conflicting interests and delicate emotions. It's also ideal for someone looking to get more visibility with the Board. So I think it would be the perfect fit for you – I've seen you get great results from some very tense meetings, and I know how much you want to make progress up the ladder.

Gillian: (*Yes!*) Thank you, Laura. That's lovely to hear. I guess you're thinking of those Draycox meetings I chaired. Yes, I was pleased with how they turned out, and it's lovely to hear you say so too. I'm also very grateful to you for thinking of me in this way. [Pausing to think]

It is a very good opportunity.....

[Pausing again]

(*No*)... and I'm also thinking of the decontamination project. It's getting me working seventy-hour weeks already, we're two weeks behind on the deadline, and I really want to turn that around. The last thing I want is having you hauled onto the news at eight a.m. to explain why the beaches around here aren't safe to swim in.

So I'm going to have to say no for now. (*Yes?*) If it can wait six months, I'd love to take up your offer. Otherwise, have you thought of John? I know he's quite passionate in this area (remember all the extra research he did on Banyard; he was working Sundays for months). He's brilliant at winning consensus too, don't you think?[11]

Notice how Gillian is genuinely pleased to receive the offer, and pauses to give the question genuine thought – which communicates how seriously she's considering it. She is clear about her No, and offers not one but two possibilities.

Excluding a topic

This is a very flexible framework for difficult discussions. It can work well when we need to make the container stronger, by focusing the discussion and excluding certain topics. Then it might look like this:

1. I know we are all keen to discuss X topic. It's very important because of Y and Z.

2. We aren't going to be considering it in this meeting/group/project, because of A and B.

3. However, it will be dealt with (at another stage/in another place/by another group/when circumstances allow, etc). Those of you who are interested will have the chance to put your views forward at that stage.

This basic form of a positive No can be used upwards as well – if your boss is wanting things which you can't or won't participate in, then the same form can be used.

Letting someone go

As a Host Leader, we will of course be making every effort to use the skills and talents of our people. Even so, it is possible that in the end we may need to go so far and close the gate on someone's involvement with the organization – and let them go. Or fire them.

A Host Leader will know the importance even in this difficult situation of helping matters to proceed as smoothly as possible. We will do whatever we can to help the person find other work and give as good a reference as possible, use contacts to find potential situations, offer time to find another position, and do our best to part on good terms. Playing tough may occasionally be necessary, but perhaps less than HR lawyers may think.

Sometimes you may even need to close down a whole organization. In these cases, it can be useful to think about helping people to move on, rituals for closing (so that there is a moment where the transition actually happens), and helping people keep in touch afterwards.

Stepping back

Stepping back is, as ever, about awareness. The gate is always there to be kept when needed, and the Host Leader will be on the lookout for signs that it may soon be time to open wider or close the gate.

The Host Leader will also have half an eye on the doorway – looking to react if someone unexpected appears. In the great tradition of hospitality, the unexpected guest is always to be welcomed in, valued and looked after – inspiration, change and new possibilities can come from the most unexpected places.

If there are people or topics which need (for now) to be excluded, then that can be one of the most challenging moments. A Host Leader is not afraid to step forward again here and make clear moves for the good of the long-term progress of the group and the endeavor.

Gatekeeper

- Take note of the thresholds to your space
- Be observant of container size – could it be changed?
- Step back and welcome people from other boundaries and spaces

- Welcome people in and establish defining routines and rituals
- Change container size – more/fewer people, bigger/smaller topic
- Be prepared to exclude people and topics – a positive No, temporarily, or even for the foreseeable future

Reflective questions

- Where are the thresholds in your organization? How do you look after them?

- What routines and rituals help people know they are in your space? How can you make more use of small regular events?

- Are your containers sometimes too big? Or too small? Where could you usefully reduce the container (for more focus) or expand (for more possibilities)?

- When do you boundary-span? When would be good times to invite new blood and ideas across your threshold?

- When was the last time you had to "close the gate" on a topic, person or group? How did you do it? What did you learn?

Key points

- ➢ Welcome newcomers across the threshold.

- ➢ Build an appropriate sense of identity and integrity.

- ➢ Use routines and rituals constructively, with good enough holding of safety.

- ➢ Keep an eye on the containers within which they are working.

- ➢ Take steps to change the container if needed – bigger or smaller, stronger or weaker.

- ➢ Boundary-span, and welcome visitors from other containers.

- ➢ Exclude where necessary – questions/topics may be easier to exclude than people.

10

Connector

"We used to think that if we knew one, we knew two, because one and one are two. We are finding that we must learn a great deal more about 'and.'"

~Arthur Eddington, astronomer, 1882–1944

 Host Leaders are connectors. They build connections between people, link people and ideas AND know when to leave them to get on with it. Think of a connector in an electrical circuit: it joins two things together and something happens that wouldn't have been possible without that connection; for example, a light comes on, we hear a sound, or a kettle boils. Similarly, the Host Leader as connector joins people together and creates the possibility of something emerging that would not have happened without the connector.

If we've initiated something, invited people to get involved and created a space for things to take place, we clearly want to create something. We want something to happen and it is likely that it wouldn't happen without people getting together. As connectors, we understand that, having brought people together, at some point we need to get out of the way, let the magic work and allow possibilities to emerge – "Light the blue touchpaper and stand back," as it said on all British fireworks when we were young.

In this chapter, we'll be looking at how connecting is a key role for a Host Leader. The role of connector is both about making the connection and also about walking away. It is not about owning the connection; rather, it is about knowing if and when to reconnect.

We're also going to explore what happens when we are naturally a connector and connecting is a way of being. By thinking like a host as a connector in different situations or contexts, we can open up new possibilities. What do you think could happen to you if you thought of yourself as a connector?

In this chapter, we will look at three levels of connector:

Level 1: Connecting with others (understanding people)
Level 2: Connecting others (connecting people and ideas)
Level 3: Everything is connected (wise connectedness).

Level 1: Connecting with others (understanding people)

Like us, you might like to be around connectors – real connectors, that is. Yes, connectors see you. They have a knack for putting people at ease. They include you, speak highly of you, get people talking, and get the party started. We're interested in how they do that. What makes the difference?

As we saw in the Gatekeeper chapter, starting at the beginning, connectors are on hand to meet and greet people on arrival. They are welcoming, settle you in, show you where to go, and do other housekeeping things like directing you to refreshments.

As Host Leaders, we can aspire to always take care to be warm and open when initiating contact with others. This is a key feature of hosting through the ages and it would be very odd if the host didn't greet you in some way. But as the host, are we always on hand to welcome people? What might be the benefit if we were?

Be interested, not interesting

Connectors are interested in you. There is a saying: "Be interested, not interesting." We've all come across hosts who prefer to be interesting. They talk about themselves all the time and don't seem to be interested in anyone else. Returning to the Disraeli Effect from Chapter 1, Disraeli was clearly a connector. Leadership guru Warren Bennis comments, "Gladstone shone but Disraeli created an environment where others could shine. The latter is the more powerful form of leadership, an adventure in which the leader is privileged to find treasure within others and put it to good use."[1] More on this later.

Good hosts connect with you and understand you apparently effortlessly. They get you talking. You talk more than they do and this can feel like there is an instant connection. This is because they listen well and acknowledge what you are saying, show empathy and demonstrate understanding.

One instant benefit of an initial connection is that it helps you start to find out about people – starting with their name. Mark recalls a startling event from his days as a student at Bristol University in the late 1970s:

> *"I was studying physics, and did chemistry as well in the first year as an option. Our organic chemistry lecturer was Dr Lionel Hart, an excellent teacher. I don't recall much of the actual learning, and passed the exams satisfactorily – I was just one of a hundred students in a large first-year course. Two years later, I paid a rare visit to the chemistry building, entered the elevator, and saw Dr Hart get in after me. 'Hello Mark, how are you?' he asked. I was stunned and staggered. Here was I, a very ordinary student from two years ago, and he remembered my name! This was undoubtedly the most important thing that ever happened to me in the chemistry department – much more relevant than ligands and free radicals. What an honor to be known and recognized by such a respected person."*

Mark wondered for a while whether he had attained some kind of notoriety but he need not have worried – it turned out that every year Dr Hart had, *by the first lecture*, memorized the names, faces, schools and even A-level grades of every student in his class. As one head of chemistry recalled,[2] "Everyone remembers Dr Hart." Because he remembered them.

Acknowledge the 'walk' of the other

One very powerful way to think about meeting other people is through the concept of their "walk." This idea was introduced to us by Jill Pearman of Mind Matters, a mental health and well-being nonprofit organization in Australia. Jill is a remarkable woman – she has a lifetime of experience in working with education for healthy living, and set up Life Education Centres, another outstanding organization focusing on educating school pupils about drug-free lifestyles, in the UK.

Jill says that if you want to take people with you and to build an environment where others can flourish and be the best they can be, you need to acknowledge them as an individual first. She talks about the "walk" – the journey being undertaken by the other, the person you are meeting and connecting with. "All too often workplaces greet people with the job title. Each individual on the planet is so much more than this and as humans we flourish and shine when our walk, our humanity is acknowledged. You can never know their walk, their experience, their journey, what they live – because it's theirs," she says.[3] "However, you *CAN* acknowledge it. If you invite people into a space where their walk can be acknowledged, all sorts of things can happen – as long as you are meeting them as a person first." Meeting them as a person, not as a representative, a region, a statistic, a token... Even if someone is coming to you as a representative or in a specific capacity, meet them as a *person* first, and be interested in their walk.

Jill pondered whether being very "other-focused" might be dangerous – that there might be a risk of losing yourself as a leader by keeping a strong attention on other people, but she now reflects, "I don't think so... I think it actually makes you stronger because it allows you to have a real understanding of someone else. It really matters to me that I am conscious of what our team is going through. I am a very busy person, but if a member of my team has something happening, I will call them and ask how it went. If you are not doing that with every member of your team, you're not going to get them to walk into the space where you want to be. You want them to own it and love it, where they can go the extra mile, where they *feel* those things that matter to them – rather than telling them."

Meeting people in their resources first

Another powerful idea about meeting comes from Insoo Kim Berg, one of the co-developers of solution-focused therapy methods and one of Mark's teachers. She always said, "Meet people in their resources first." As a therapist, Insoo would usually be meeting people who had been diagnosed with problems. Starting the conversation at the point of the problem was, however, not at all a part of her style. She would be very observant and be on the lookout for examples of their "resources" – strengths, useful qualities, interests, support, willingness – and was equally keen to find moments to let people know she had noticed these aspects (which were typically never noticed, let alone discussed as a priority, by other clinicians). This idea connects with the Disraeli effect we mentioned at the start of the book. Disraeli must have been a great Connector.

Have I met you before?

We encounter many opportunities for meeting and connecting with people. These encounters might be represented on a spectrum of previous contact or past experience. This could span a range from, say, the meeting of a stranger whom we are unlikely to ever meet again, to first meeting a new contact, meeting with a work colleague, through to a longstanding friend whom we've known for many years. Thinking like a connector helps us maximize every opportunity.

Connectors are good at picking up clues about people's "walk." They look and observe – what are they wearing, what clues can you gather from them about whether they have had an easy journey or a tough one, where are they heading for, what are they looking for, what connections you already have (common acquaintances, former colleagues, places of work, places you have lived or visited, common interests…). All these build connection quickly.

Connectors are open to new encounters; they are curious; they know strangers come bearing gifts; they connect quickly, almost instantly, noticing and acknowledging people's "walk"; and they know when to connect them to others and move on.

Catch people doing things right

When working with people in our teams, it can be so easy to begin on the slippery slope of noticing what they are *NOT* doing, rather than seeing them in terms of their resources and remembering what they do *well*. Helen has seen many examples of this, the starkest of which is a boss who described a new employee as a star, saying, "We could do with more like him." Within six months, the same boss was describing him as lazy. What had happened? Helen's observation was that the boss hadn't taken the time to stay connected with him, to understand him, and as a result he didn't feel listened to or valued.

It is an ongoing requirement, catching people doing things right, noticing their resources. How much better is it to receive feedback on what we are doing well, rather than only on when things go wrong? Of course, when we are busy and over-stretched ourselves, we often aren't thinking about how other people tick or why they are behaving the way they are. We are focused on getting done what we need to do, having enough money to pay the wages, surviving. As we saw in the Space Creator chapter, we need to create the head space, spend time "in the kitchen," to reflect on what we know about our people and how best to work with them. Even something as simple as starting every meeting with a round of "what is going well" can make a huge difference.

Level 2: Connecting others (connecting people and ideas)

Hosts connect with their guests – and they also connect their guests to each other. This can be very valuable indeed to leaders and yet it is not done nearly as well or as often as it could be. Through their ability to understand you quickly – and no doubt with a little homework as well – connectors also know who else to connect you with. Let's start with an example from Helen:

> "At a recent event, as a guest on a table, the host said to the person next to me, 'Have you told Helen about your course in Cornwall?' No, he hadn't. I was intrigued so Anthony proceeded to tell me about his course... in clay plastering!! Of course, the host knew that I was in the process of renovating a property, and so she connected us based on something she knew about each of us, something we could usefully talk about – he could share his experience with me and I would be very interested. The thing is, when we make these introductions, we never know where they may lead. I now know someone who has a very unique skill in the North of England; my builder does renovation projects; I'm connecting with others who are interested in property and buildings; I'm connecting with other tradespeople, and so on."

Without the host acting as connector, that possibility might never have been uncovered. It was always there but it could have been missed. Perhaps what's more to the point is that, other than having a good night with happy guests, there was nothing in it for the host to make the connection, but she did... and left Helen and Anthony to it. Lit the blue touchpaper and stood back...

Connection: creating something from (almost) nothing

It has been said that love, attention and connection are some of the few things that grow by being given away. When you connect two or more people, you never know what might be possible.

For example, an essential part of a leadership program run by Helen for owner/managers of growing businesses was the peer-to-peer element. It is widely acknowledged that being the leader of a business can be a lonely place. There often isn't anyone else to talk to, share with or learn from. The program brought groups of twenty-five business owners together to work and learn together over a ten-month period. It was essential for Helen, as the program leader, to connect the group from the beginning and then step back and allow relationships to develop.

Helen reflects on what was required:

> *"Investing time in the initial connecting paid huge dividends. Whenever I bring a group together, I start by thinking about their 'walk' – What do I know about them? How do they come to be here? Who are they connected to? I always put myself in their shoes – What will they be feeling? What else might be going on for them? What might they need? I take care over the details – name badges, refreshments, room layout, meeting and greeting, etc. Whenever I can, I will be there to connect with people when they arrive and then to connect them to others. I might introduce them to someone with whom they have a mutual connection, geography; e.g., they are based in the same area, or because there may be a mutual business interest. Sometimes there is no obvious connection; they are simply someone else on the same program. I am very open with them and presuppose they will be open with each other. So when I get them talking to each other in an exercise, it never crosses my mind that they won't engage. People often comment how much our groups share and so quickly."*

As well as benefiting from the program objectives of leadership development and business growth, many of the participants did business together *AND* new ventures were formed. Whilst some of the results undoubtedly came about through elements of the program, the investment in encouraging them to build relationships and really connect with one another created a strong foundation for this to happen. The business owners were open to possibilities, and when opportunities presented themselves, they were ready to take them. Where once they might have seen competition and a need to protect, they saw collaboration and the possibility of more for all.

As a Host Leader, being a connector can make all the difference to the commitment and engagement of the team. Traditionally, leaders, particularly hero leaders, acted as if they were the ones who had to have all the answers, as if no one else would know what to do. For some followers, this is great – they like to be told what to do, and to be given clear instructions. For many, however, it means that their curiosity and creativity are compromised. Connectors bring people together, introduce them to each other and to the reason for bringing them together: a problem to be solved, a challenge, an opportunity.

The next thing the connector does is leave people to get on with it – whether they physically leave, or stay quiet and allow the team to work things out and support them in implementing their ideas. It makes a great difference, and yet often it is very hard for the leader who may be tempted to micromanage the team. Perhaps it is hard to let go, especially if the outcome is not quite what you expected. Of course, at that point, the leader always has the opportunity to step in *BUT* only if absolutely necessary, and they know that they must tread carefully.

Hosting around the world: All together for a South American asado

The *asado* is a regular part of social life in Argentina. It's a barbecue event, but with a strong social context. In South America, the *parrilla*, the outdoor grill, is not wheeled out of the garage; it is built onto many homes, and forms a key focus for hosting and conversation. It is *NOT* simply a meal, although food is an important part of the proceedings.

Things will start as the guests begin to arrive. Some will have brought additional food; others will help with preparing salads and accompaniments to the grilled fare. The charcoal will be lit, the slow process of building the fire to perfection starts, some bottles are opened ... And people join together as one group to take time, connect, interact and enjoy. It's not like a cocktail party, with people split into small groups – there is definitely a whole-group feel to the proceedings. Everyone is engaged, whether in preparing, slicing, talking, encouraging and supporting – this is a slow-food phenomenon.

The host – usually a man, it has to be said – is in charge of grilling the meat, the centerpiece of the gathering. Everyone is complimentary and supportive of the host, who cooks the meat in their particular style. However, a good host knows who likes their meat rare or well done, and who prefers a vegetarian alternative. Argentinean colleague Veronica de Andrés told us, "If people put ten percent of the effort they make for an asado into leadership, we would be in a completely different paradigm!"

The social butterfly

Helen reflects on her experience as a connector:

> *"'Helen was there, doing her social butterfly again.' This was a comment made to a good friend of mine after a formal dinner dance held in the region where I worked. It was an annual event for employees and their partners, a highlight in the social calendar. The great and the good were there representing all corners of the region and all ranks and roles. To be fair, my role spanned the region so I knew many people there. Yet the words still took me by surprise: that someone noticed what I'd been doing – I wasn't even aware of it myself – and made such a comment. So I asked myself, what is a social butterfly?"*

When we think of butterflies, we think of graceful little creatures that flutter about in the summer sunshine, landing on pretty, colorful flowers. We think of their exquisite markings, delicate wings and constant movement, save for their resting on occasional flowers. They fly, hover, land and take off again moving quickly from place to place. They don't stay long in any one place. They are pollinators – increasing the productivity of the plants they visit. Helen continues:

> *"Reflecting on myself at the dinner, I knew many people in the room, all seated at different tables. I made a point of seeking people out and visiting the various tables. I spent time with people engaged in conversation. Like the butterfly, I could be seen fluttering around from table to table, sometimes resting longer at certain tables, going back to my place from time to time only to take off again when I spotted someone else I knew."*

What is the benefit of encountering a social butterfly? They make us feel connected, create a sense of belonging, make us feel recognized. Social butterflies also connect us to others in the room, expanding our networks. Social butterflies are interested in us, leave us feeling we matter. They remember things about us and share positive stories about us with others, presenting us in a good light. When a social butterfly introduces us to somebody else, they know what we should speak about. They know about both of us and connect us with something we have in common, an opportunity or a need one of us has that the other can satisfy.

A Host Leader knows the value of connecting others – acting as a pollinator and increasing the chances of something greater than the sum of the parts happening.

Level 3: Everything is connected (wise connectedness)

"When we try to pick out something by itself, we find it hitched to everything else in the universe."

~John Muir, father of the USA National Parks

John Muir was wise to see that, in the end, everything is connected. This is not to say that we can't treat things as being units as a matter of convenience, but in the end that's what our boundaries are – a matter of convenience.

Muir was not referring here to some kind of ethereal force, some mysterious "field" binding everything. In a complex system (like the world in which we live), connections and interactions can mean that a change in one part of the system can lead to unexpected changes elsewhere. Even if the "mechanism" of the system is understood, the precise details of every fluctuation cannot be calculated in advance. Happy synchronicities and unintended consequences are inevitable results.

We wrote in the opening chapter about how this plays out in our organizations these days with VUCA problems and Grint's "wicked" problems. This all sounds like a scary place to be – if we can't control everything, how are we to cope? Yet this is further evidence of the need for a different way of thinking about leadership. "Command and control" or "predict and control" no longer hold the solutions to today's problems. It turns out that many traditions have been grappling with this for millennia. Here are a few pointers.

Raising awareness

The key to finding and making use of unexpected connections is first of all to *notice* them. The happy synchronicities are there all the time; it's just that we don't notice them. When our heads are full of everything we have to do, let alone what everybody else should be doing, and we are trying to think several steps ahead, our minds are too cluttered to notice connections. There's no space for awareness of synchronicities. Practices such as mindfulness, meditation and relaxation can help us to create the conditions in our minds for new realizations to begin to dawn. The benefits of such practices are becoming clearer – even such ancient establishments as the British Parliament are now offering mindfulness courses to busy lawmakers.

Broaden and build

One way of improving our capacity to notice useful changes and connections is to use Barbara Fredrickson's "broaden and build" hypothesis.[4] Fredrickson is one of the leaders in positive psychology and has researched the impacts of positive emotions. Her findings are that noticing and engaging in positive experiences not only feels good, but also broadens our ability to think creatively and expansively. This puts us into a great place for building progress and better futures. While there have been some debates about the precise figures in Fredrickson's work, the basic conclusions are robust and support Mark's previous work in Solutions Focus – finding what works is not only logically useful but also emotionally valuable.

Know what would be useful to discover

When we know what we're looking for, we are much more likely to see it. In psychology, this is called the "Frequency Illusion" – once we have thought about something (buying a new car, for example), we start to notice examples of the same car driving past. They were driving past all the time, of course, but we didn't notice them because we didn't know they were important.

In the *User's Guide to the Future* chapter, we talked about the importance of knowing both long-term hopes and short-term "signs of progress." It is the "signs of progress" thinking that can be really useful here – by knowing what would be a great sign of progress, we can be alert to it even if it shows up unexpectedly.

The natural world of connection

Being a connector is our true nature and we've lost sight of it. In today's world, with terrible experiences such as 9/11, a world recession and devastating natural disasters, a culture of fear is evident. People have become focused on themselves, survival and self-protection. This has taken over, even though we know this approach isn't working and we need to return to our true nature and be connectors.

Robert Greenleaf, the key developer of Servant-Leadership, wrote that the essence of leadership is the desire to serve one another and to serve something beyond ourselves, a higher purpose.[5] We propose that the host-guest relationship shines an interesting light on this wide question. The only thing is – are we the hosts or the guests?

The Host Leader recognizes the implications of interconnectedness: the inadequacy of command and control leadership; the value of tentative (experimental) small steps; and the importance of awareness and recognition of what is being sought.

Thinking like a connector

Being a good connector means thinking like one. We have been studying the kinds of thinking that seem to interfere with people making connections, and we believe there are often three great misunderstandings at work:

- I'll give you something, but only if you give me something

- If I give you something, you won't need me anymore

- If I give you something, I'll have less of it

Connectors know that these are *mis*understandings and work instead from three different standpoints:

- If I give you something, you are more likely to give me something

- If I give you something, our relationship is more valuable, not less

- If I give you something (like knowledge, love, care, interest), then we *BOTH* have more of it

Let's examine these three ideas.

If I give you something, you are more likely to give me something

Dr Ivan Misner is the founder of BNI, the worldwide business networking organization. With almost seven thousand chapters worldwide, members share their business goals, contacts, leads and referrals with each other. This simple action generates business – an astonishing $6.5 billion in a single year as we write.

Ivan has built BNI on the principle of "Givers Gain®." He is very aware that the usual assumption of sharing – I'll give you something *IF* you give me something – is deeply flawed. If I wait for you to give me something... and you are doing the same thing... then guess what? Neither of us will ever give the other anything at all! Someone has to start – to go first, to give, to connect, to show some faith in the other.

Of course, giving something to someone is only a good thing if the recipient actually values what is given. The Host Leader will be focusing on meeting people and finding out about their "walk," and so will already be in a position to know what might be useful.

So, the idea of Givers Gain® – and the idea of leading in generosity – is of course an idea we can only apply to ourselves. If we wait around and point the finger at others for not having a Givers Gain® attitude (or whatever), then we are not applying this way of thinking. What we are saying is that they don't seem to give enough – so we're not going to give them anything until they do!

Hosting around the world: Giving it all at the Potlatch

Perhaps the ultimate example of a giving culture was the Potlatch tradition, part of the culture of the indigenous tribes of the Pacific Northwest of what is now Canada and the USA. At a potlatch, the host would hold a huge party and proceed to give all their possessions away. The bigger the giveaway, the more respect and prestige they accumulated. These ceremonies would often happen to celebrate births, marriages, deaths, namings and other rites of passage. Was the host left destitute after these events? No – they would have won great respect, others in the community would help, and there would be someone else giving another potlatch soon anyway. This custom was banned by the coloniz-ing powers in the late 1800s, who considered it "a worse than useless custom" that was seen as wasteful, unproductive, and contrary to civilized values.[6] Some have noted that the settlers' culture of trading for money is undermined if everyone can get things for nothing. The ban was fiercely resisted, and was eventually repealed in 1951 – but not before the indigenous cultures had been changed forever.

If I give you something, our relationship is more valuable, not less

Connectors don't just give things – and connections – in the hope of getting something back. They also know the power of generosity in building relationships. It's not simply giving material things of course – there is much else that is valuable:

- Connections
- Information
- Attention
- Love
- Care
- Credit
- Acknowledgement

Some people worry about helping people to be more resourceful and self-reliant – because they will then go on to be better, leave the nest and fly away. Much has been written about how good leaders will focus on developing new and better leaders (rather than followers). When we invest in relationships, we never know what is going to come back and where from. We invest in developing a member of our team who goes on to leave the organization. It can feel like such a blow – the time we've put in and the time to find a replacement – yet what comes back might be good press about the company as a good employer, a good company to work for. We never know what things will lead to.

Another concept which has gained popularity since the film of the same name is "Pay It Forward" – again about having a connecting or giving mindset. In the novel and subsequent film, a social studies teacher gives his class an assignment to devise and put into action a plan that will change the world for the better. One student's plan is a charitable program based on the networking of good deeds. He calls his plan "Pay It Forward," which means the recipient of a favor does a favor for three others rather than paying the favor back. Of course, what is interesting is unraveling the links and connections between the donors and recipients of the favors: how everything is connected and we never know how things that we give will come back to us.

If I give you something (like knowledge, love, care, interest), then we BOTH have more of it

Connectors are dedicated to working with an abundance mentality. The opposite – a scarcity mentality – results from days when food and goods were scarce, and had to be hoarded to prevent the family from starvation or worse.

However, the kinds of things shared by connectors – connections, links, ideas, credit, attention and love – do not shrink by being shared. They increase – I still have my connection, and now you have it too. So you have more than you did… and, miraculously, so do I.

Let's briefly look at how the mathematics of connections works. Suppose we both have networks of a hundred people. When we meet and connect, our networks both increase by one. Not much. However, I also have the possibility of connecting with your network of a hundred. Better.

But what happens when I, as a Host Leader, connect two other people? Let's assume they both have networks of a hundred. By making one single connection, I have opened up the direct possibility of connections between any of the two networks of a hundred – which is ten thousand possible connections. Much better. It's this kind of process that makes the online business networking site LinkedIn so successful and useful of course. The art of making good use of these potential connections is another whole topic (and another whole book) in itself. As a Host Leader, we know the power and value of making and expanding on these connections – among our guests and invitees.

Stepping back

What does stepping back mean for the Connector? As so often, this role can start with stepping back to notice what kinds of connections might be useful. Being open, being aware.

Then the chance comes to make a connection – either for ourselves or (even better) between other people. That's the time to step forward, make the links, share something valuable.

And then … step back again. The connection is made – butterfly away, let things emerge, let people get on with it. Not all connections will flourish – indeed, we've seen some for which we had high hopes come to nothing, while other surprisingly odd connections have turned into very valuable and key relationships. It can take years for a connection to show some value – and in that time, of course, we might think it's come to nothing. Trusting that things will develop in a useful way is a valuable skill for a Host Leader. And of course, we can always step forward to give another nudge if that seems to be the right thing to do.

There is a risk of stepping back too soon – before connections have been made and people are ready to move together. Mark was once invited to join a very exciting movement at the height of the banking crisis, one which was going to really say that "enough was enough and it was time for change." There was a nice logo, interesting plans were mooted, and anything seemed possible. Many interesting and well-connected people gathered in a London meeting room, where the host invited us to introduce ourselves and then said… "What do you want to do?" Mark could feel the energy go from the room – we had come together ready to help to do this thing (whatever it was), and we just weren't ready to *invent* the thing. Perhaps with a little more shape, things might have turned out differently – a Gatekeeper helping to work within a more tightly defined container would also have helped. Anyway, not much else was heard from this particular group, which was a shame.

That's the dance of the Host Leader – stepping forward and back, acting and leaving alone, connecting but not dominating, thinking of possibilities rather than certainties.

When the sign of life is in your face

In closing, let us return to the very first moment of connection – the moment someone comes through the door and into the space. Verse 35 of the Tao Te Ching[7] cuts to the heart of this moment:

> *If the sign of life is in your face*
> *He who responds to it*
> *Will feel secure and fit*
> *As when, in a friendly place,*
> *Sure of hearty care,*
> *A traveler gladly waits.*
> *Though it may not taste like food*
> *And he may not see the fare*
> *Or hear a sound of plates,*
> *How endless it is and how good!*

The sign of life – the glance of recognition and acknowledgement – is the start of everything. We know the difference between entering a busy café (say) with no acknowledgement – and entering to a welcoming glance from the host. Even though the actual food and drink may not be on their way, we can feel "secure and fit" that we are somehow in a place where good things will happen. So, too, does the Host Leader know how to cultivate good connections in the team, so that good things can happen in due course.

Connector

- Look out for not-yet-connected people
- Look for opportunities to build connections between others
- Be aware of connection all around

- Connect with new people and their "walk" (Level 1)
- Connect others – the social butterfly (Level 2)
- Respond to new awareness with openness – perhaps a new call is forming? (Level 3)

Reflective questions

- How good are you at connecting with new people? Who was the last new person with whom you forged a continuing connection?

- How can you be even more interested in the "walk" of the other? How might that help you connect more strongly?

- Who could you usefully connect to someone else, right now?

- What unexpected or unusual themes might you use to connect others? (Helen mentioned clay-plastering above)

- How have you recently noticed the connectivity in the universe?

- How could you be even more open to the unexpected and the different?

Key Points

Three levels of connecting:

>   Level 1: Connecting with others – meeter and greeter

       • Have the "sign of life" in your face – connect right away
       • Be interested in the walk of the other
       • Greet like a host

>   Level 2: Connecting others to each other – social butterfly

       • Connections create something from nothing
       • Think like a connector – go first, be generous, build relationships
       • Keep moving – butterfly onwards and let people get on with it

>   Level 3: Everything is connected

       • Be calm and clear, to notice useful connections and possibilities
       • Broaden and build
       • Enjoy and wonder at the massive connectivity in the world

11

Co-Participator

"Guests are carrying precious gifts with them, which they are eager to reveal to a receptive host."

~Henri Nouwen, Reaching Out[1]

 Our final role for a Host Leader is Co-Participator. Co-Participators initiate and provide *AND* join in along with everyone else. It is no surprise that hosts initiate proceedings and provide for their guests. But do they always join in too?

In hosting terms, this is absolutely obvious. When we are invited for dinner, we expect the host to not only serve us with food, but eat the same food with us. It would be very strange to go to a dinner party and have the host eat in the kitchen! And if we got the idea that they were hidden away in there eating better food than what we were getting, we'd be insulted.

Not only that; hosting etiquette the world over demands that the host serve their guests first. How would it be if the host served themselves a generous plateful, looked disappointedly around and said, "Sorry, there doesn't seem to be any left for you...?" In hosting terms, this is a clear expectation. In leadership terms, it doesn't seem to be so clear. When the news is full of stories about bank CEOs who appear to have eaten heartily in terms of massive bonuses and taken their organizations beyond the brink of bankruptcy, we might think that the ancient values of relationship and hospitality have well and truly been abandoned.

We think it's time to bring them back.

In this chapter, we'll be looking at the Host Leader's co-participating role. Whilst co-participating is about joining in with the guests, it is not about joining in to the detriment of knowing what is going on all around and responding as we deem appropriate.

Returning to the dinner party example, perhaps this is why guests often choose to congregate in the kitchen – we want to be with the host, engaging with the host, rather than sitting in a different room. On the occasions when, as guests, we have been ushered into another room, banished from the kitchen, there can be that awkward silence; something's missing. That something is the host Co-Participator, joining in with the guests and at the same time noticing when glasses need refilling, being aware of timing and being open to suggestions that might make the evening go with even more of a bang.

Co-participating achieves so much more than leaving people to get on with it themselves. It builds effective relationships *AND* the credibility of the leader. This truly engages people *AND* ensures you, as the leader, know what's going on. Being a Co-Participator can give you different perspectives... if you are open to them.

Co-participating helps us uncover people's gifts; it makes people want to reveal them, as in our opening quote from Henri Nouwen. Look out for the variety of gifts people may bring in the rest of the chapter.

Before we delve deeper into the role of Co-Participator, thinking as a host, let's remind ourselves where we are: we've initiated something, an event or a project maybe; we've invited people to get involved; created an appropriate space and minded the gate; as people have arrived, we've connected them and now the event or project is getting underway, we are thinking about how the Host Leader might cooperate with the assembled guests. We will then look at the Co-Participator role:

- In the spotlight

- With the guests

- In the gallery

The spotlight of leadership versus the alongside-ness of participation

It is a tough job, balancing what to do and where to be at all times, having an eye on what needs to be done and what is happening at the same time. A Co-Participator is active in the space as well as being the "leader." They are participating in conversations, having useful interactions, identifying possible opportunities and connections, yet at the same time guests feel a sense of assurance that everything is under control, being well led and managed; all is happening perfectly.

This is not to say that we should aim to be "just one of the guys" – leadership brings the need to be different and slightly apart. Here, we are showing the advantages when that includes joining in from time to time. This is an answer to the problem of "executive isolation," raised by Harvard Business School.[2] Those around a senior executive attempt to leverage their time by only letting in certain topics. This is done with good intentions of efficiency, but it leaves the senior person adrift of the rich variety of developments in their organization.

The following example, of a site foreman delivering his daily message to the workers on-site, illustrates what can happen if we are not a Co-Participator. This particular day, the boss of the whole company happened to be on-site and observed the morning meeting. As he watched and listened, he realized that what the foreman was telling the workers to do wouldn't work. What's more, he could see that the workers also knew that what they were being told to do wouldn't work. Not one of them spoke out, and off they went to get on with their day's work. The boss observed how people undermined the foreman by doing exactly what he told them to do. If the foreman had had more of an appetite for co-participating, he would have seen much more quickly the impact of his behavior in terms of slowing up the work. The boss, in his role of Co-Participator, was now in a position to realize that there was an issue emerging and begin to deal with it.

How might being a Co-Participator help?

Building the credibility of the leader

In our experience, the best leaders seem to adopt an approach along the lines of, "We all have our roles to do but underneath we are no different," and, "I don't have all the answers – my job is to engage with those who might." It is an approach that is rooted in humility. As a result, people feel valued and that their contribution is valued. Contrast this with the site foreman above.

Providing different perspectives

As a Co-Participator, we can talk with people at all levels. Indeed, we see it as imperative as that's how we find out what's really going on. We learn where there are potential problems or delays and how things could be better. Think of the popularity of TV shows such as *Back to the Floor* or *Undercover Boss*. NatWest Bank have recently announced that relationship managers will spend time each year in customers' businesses, which will provide them with a different perspective on what it's like to run a business and hence what businesses really need from their bank.

If we actually believe we don't have all the answers, then this is how we start to *find* the answers – engage with people who are doing the job or at least check out whether our ideas might work. Better still, empower them to come up with the answers and implement them. Our site foreman would have saved a lot of time and trouble if he had been more of a Co-Participator.

Enhancing relationships

Engaging people, asking their opinions, and seeking their input enhances relationships. Joining in with people shows we are all the same, we are on the same side. Contrast that with the boss who had a separate elevator taking him directly from the car park to his office precisely so he didn't have to come into contact with anyone. What did that say about the importance of relationships?

By being a Co-Participator, we achieve way more buy-in from the team. People will actually come and tell us when something could be better or won't work and they can see a better way. Again, how differently it could have turned out for our site foreman.

The unseen benefits of co-participating

The actual benefits of being a Co-Participator will outweigh all of these as we can't know what possibilities will emerge from the interactions we have as we join in with people. As a Host Leader, we organize for people to come together and then, as we join in with our guests, prepare to be surprised by what emerges.

What do Co-Participators do?

Let us start with a reminder of our four positions for Host Leaders:

- In the spotlight
- In the gallery
- With the guests
- In the kitchen

Co-Participators will value their time "with the guests" and "in the gallery." Being in the spotlight is about taking on a special role with attention and command. Many leaders think that this is where leaders can and *SHOULD* act. Being in the kitchen is about private and intimate spaces, where truths can be told and hard questions considered. Some, in our experience, are so used to being in the spotlight that they find little time for even kitchen-based reflection and nurturing, let alone the other elements.

In the spotlight

Stepping forward – to serve others first

This is a principle that holds true in many different situations. It would be unusual for a host to eat first or for the organizer of an event to take their seat first. This is one point where host and Servant-Leadership traditions are in full accord. Just as it is poor hosting to serve yourself first and take too much food, the Host Leader is very careful to ensure that people have what they need first, before looking after themselves. This is a time when the focus is on others.

Hosting around the world: Providing for all in the Sikh langar

In Sikh temples, or gurdwaras, around the world, we find the tradition of the langar – the kitchen where food is served to all the visitors (without distinction of background) for free. Usually, only vegetarian food is served, to ensure that all people, regardless of their dietary restrictions, can eat as equals. Started by the first guru, Guru Nanak, this tradition is designed to uphold the principle of equality regardless of caste, creed or anything else – a truly revolutionary concept in the caste-layered world of sixteenth-century India. Langars can be absolutely huge operations – the Golden Temple in Amritsar serves up to a hundred thousand meals daily, and the kitchen works for twenty hours out of every twenty-four.[3]

Not the Big Shot

One way not to be a Host Leader is to play the big shot. Big-shot leaders parachute in with all eyes upon them, make a speech that someone else wrote for them, and then disappear off again before anyone can get too close or ask awkward questions. As a Host Leader, we may have to make short visits, but they will be focused on finding out about what's happening, making contact with people and doing what we can to ensure those people have what they need – in terms of resources, and in terms of attention.

The first time Mark met US success guru and author Jack Canfield was at a conference in Liverpool. Jack was top of the bill, the keynote speaker. Just the previous week, a profile of him in the British press had painted him as something of a big shot. The reality was very different and much more "hostly." Having given the keynote speech, Jack stayed for the next two days and participated to the full. He even identified a cozy corner in the hotel where he could sit, and positively invited the participants to come and take a few moments to join him to discuss whatever they wished. Several times Mark passed this corner; sometimes Jack was deep in conversation, on other occasions he was sitting quietly and waiting for another passerby.

Hosting around the world: Serving others first in the Army

The British Army knows all about putting others first. The Army's leadership anthology – a book until recently not available through the regular book trade but given to all officer students at the prestigious Sandhurst Academy – is even called *Serve To Lead*.[4] The book is filled with inspiring passages about leadership, from historic times to the present day.

At the end of the book, there is a single paragraph, contained within a box. It's entitled "The Short Version of This Book," and reads as follows:

> *"Unselfishness, as far as you are concerned, means simply this – you will put first the honour and interests of your country and your regiment; next, you will put the safety, well-being and comfort of your men; and last – and last all the time – you will put your own interest, your own safety, your own comfort."*
>
> ~Field Marshal Sir William Slim (1957)

This is very striking. From afar, we usually associate military leadership with command and control. And indeed it is, in some ways – at moments of great duress, people need to act quickly and skillfully, in line with their training. But what kind of relationship must be built up so that men will put their lives in peril instantly and without question? A very strong relationship!

Perhaps the ultimate example of an Army officer putting himself first in recent times is the story of Lt Colonel Herbert "H" Jones. During the Falklands War of 1982, he was in command of 2nd Battalion The Parachute Regiment (2 PARA), one of the elite regiments known for their toughness. Jones found himself pinned down with his men by an enemy gun position. Judging that there was no escape, he led his men in a charge on the enemy, during which he lost his life. The enemy surrendered shortly afterwards, and Jones was posthumously awarded the Victoria Cross, the UK's highest award for bravery. In the words of his official VC citation:

> *"The devastating display of courage by Colonel Jones had completely undermined [the enemy's] will to fight further. Thereafter the momentum of the attack was rapidly regained, Darwin and Goose Green were liberated, and the battalion released the local inhabitants unharmed and forced the surrender of some 1,200 of the enemy.[5]"*

In the Army, this translates into practice through the idea of looking after your men before you look after yourself. The result of this is that you get well taken care of in return by your people. Looking after your people before looking after yourself engenders loyalty, people who will go the extra mile for you, who will put in the extra effort when it's needed – say, to meet a pressing deadline, service a peak in demand or support another team who are stretched to their limits.

With the guests

Stepping back – to join in and eat the same food

Having created the space, invited the people and ensured they have what they need, the next task for the Host Leader is to join in. Eat the same food; play a full part in the event; be seen to be playing a supporting role as well as a lead role. The host also joins in along with everyone else, mingling, chatting, getting to know people, hearing their views on a topic.

This can extend to being "with the customers," to see more clearly how people actually use and engage with your products and services. It's one thing to see a trained technician use a gadget in the lab; quite another to see an ordinary Joe or Joanne grappling with the same product in their kitchen or backyard.

We are often surprised at how reluctant some leaders are to co-participate – like the aforementioned CEO who had a private elevator from the underground car park to his office suite – precisely so he didn't have to walk through the main offices. He claimed that people would only want to talk to him, and this would be a distraction from their work. We say he didn't realize the power of being seen to be part of the same organization as his workers.

A good example of balancing the "initiate and provide" and joining in along with everyone else can be found in Camila Batmanghelidjh, founder of Kids Company and included in BBC Woman's Hour's Top 100 Most Powerful Women in the UK. In a recent article, she is quoted as saying, "All I've done is galvanize the six hundred staff, eleven thousand volunteers, thousands of supporters, companies who volunteer with us and communities who come together around these kids." Clearly she initiates and provides on a vast scale. One of the ways she joins in along with everyone else is "she eats all her meals at

Kids Company," an example of staying close to what's happening and staying connected.

Indeed, eating with people is a great opportunity for co-participation. In UK schools, we are seeing a return to communal eating of hot food prepared on the premises ("school dinners") which offers all kinds of opportunities for learning and interaction. This is so different from each child bringing in a packed lunch – often of unhealthy food – and eating it in competition with their peers. School food advocate Henry Dimbleby offered an insight into how not eating together results in missed opportunities. He was visiting a school and found all the staff eating their sandwiches in the staff room. He enquired about what the pupils were doing, and was told they were in their own dining room. "I went there once…" said one of the teachers. "Some of them can't even use a fork properly." "So why aren't you there teaching them?" he mused… What an opportunity wasted.

Step back to encourage others to move

Some very passionate and energetic managers struggle at first to see the benefit of joining in, of being one of the team, of doing the photocopying. However, as we learn to be Host Leaders, the many upsides of thinking this way become clear.

Stepping back and playing a more minor role for a while allows lots of things to happen:

It has the effect of offering others the chance to step forward, to show what they can do. It can be very hard to step forward with a boss who never steps back – it can look as if you're trying to take over, or it can feel like our ideas are not listened to. The boss has all the answers, does things his or her way, so why bother? By stepping back, a Host Leader can give their people the chance to lead while they see what happens and can keep an eye on the situation. It provides an opportunity for people to reveal their gifts – so stay alert to the possibilities on show.

It gives us a great opportunity to meet our people in a different way – more intimate, close up, with less pressure on all of us. We can meet them individually and in small groups, build relationships, find out what they think, what their hopes and concerns are.

Hosting around the world: Building participation
with the Tummeler

Tummeler (sometimes spelled tummler) is a Yiddish word for a particular form of entertainer. Their role is to get everyone involved in the communal activities at a party. They can't stop or go home until everyone is up and dancing, or participating in whatever way. A Tummeler was in use in the mid-twentieth century as a feature of events on the borscht circuit, a network of Jewish clubs around the Catskill Mountains of upstate New York in the USA. It has the same roots as the word "tumble."

Many projects these days seem to be implemented to a point at which everyone is ready, or at least equipped, to join in. That is the precise moment when those responsible for the project may walk away, thinking that their job is done. That's the time when the Tummeler comes into their own – actively drawing people in, getting them to participate, even provoking them. And the job is not done until everyone is up and dancing... The first few followers are totally vital – if no one is dancing, it gets to be very hard work being a Tummeler or indeed a host.

When are the times you've seen the importance of a Tummeler? Or sorely felt the need for such a character?

Being the support act

As the support act, the question we ask ourselves is "How can I best support my people?" Imagine the time when a critical project is coming to a head. People have been working on it for months and there is an important event or milestone imminent. As a Co-Participator, rather than step in and take over – and probably cause chaos in the process – there will likely be some tasks you could do that would really support the project team.

Mark worked in the electricity-generation industry early in his career. A board member was due to give evidence at a power plant planning inquiry, and went the day before to visit the hard-working team who were presenting the organization's case for a new plant. As usual, the team were working late into the night. After midnight, his preparations completed, the board member asked, "What can I do to help?" One of the secretaries – the most junior member of the team – said, "Well, this photocopying needs to be done." (This was some time ago...) So he went off and did it. Everyone else was working hard on jobs requiring detailed knowledge, so he did what was there to be done – and, of course, won huge respect from his team for doing it.

Being the support act is not about taking things away from people. A manager recently recounted the story of a new procedure that was required in the area of the business she was responsible for. This new procedure was clearly within her remit but her leader took it from her. His actions had such a detrimental effect on the manager: she felt undermined, not valued and confused. Contrast that with asking, "What can I best do to help?" and supporting her to devise and implement the new procedure, which would have had such a positive effect.

Being the support act shows you trust your people and demonstrates your confidence in them. It also means you spend time on the things the business really needs you to do, rather than those things that others can do.

In the gallery

Pinch points

Small things make a big difference when hosting. Anticipating needs is a key part of that. Hosts notice things – like a facilitator who notices when people are putting on an extra layer of clothing and responds by adjusting the heating controls at the next opportunity.

Harry Murray is Chairman of the award-winning Lucknam Park hotel in the beautiful Wiltshire countryside near Bath. Described by his peers in the British hotel business as the epitome of the host, Harry is very clear about the need for Host Leaders to co-participate.

Harry introduced us to the concept of "pinch points." These are times when, as the hotel manager, he is always present, even though his presence is not strictly required:

> *"Find the pinch points, the critical moments, and be around at that time (so you are in a position to step forward if needed). For example, suppose the hotel is hosting a wedding – when the bride comes down the stairs in her lovely gown with everyone gathered in the hall to greet her ... you need to be there. When everyone sits down at the reception, when the couple cut the cake... you need to be there. Not in the front row or taking the limelight, but present so you can offer support to both the couple and the staff, and jump in if there is a need."*[6]

"Pinch points" is a very useful concept. When are the pinch points in *your* organization? The key times when things should be okay (if you've made your preparations well), but you can gain a lot by still being there and visible.

In a workplace, there will be pinch points in terms of meeting turnaround times, order fulfillment, delivering customer orders, production lines, handover between departments and many others.

At pinch points, the Host Leader is stepped back but ready to step forward should it be required. The balance is about *when* to step forward. Stepping forward too soon could undermine a member of your team, and stepping forward a split second too late could result in disaster.

Back to the floor

Going "back to the floor" is very much a gallery activity. Going back to the floor affords the opportunity to spend time on the job with people in different areas. Given the right mindset, the leader can gather a wealth of intelligence about what is really happening in different areas.

In a previous role, Helen was responsible for helping managers improve the levels of customer service afforded to customers in their branch. External measures of the service provided were reported to the branch by way of mystery shoppers and customer questionnaires. Very often, a branch manager could not see why their scores were as they were. By picking up the reports and various other branch indicators and sitting amongst the customer service teams, evidence for the scores soon became apparent. Helen could then help the manager see what was happening and work with the manager to identify ways to improve the service.

As a Co-Participator, when you are participating in a back-to-the-floor-type activity, people will talk to you about what they are doing, what frustrates them, what challenges arise, what could be better. There is so much new awareness and learning to be gained from spending time in this position.

The idea of management as a profession is relatively recent. For someone who has come into management as a career, spending time on the floor is an ideal opportunity to learn about what goes on and how it is done. Alternatively, if the manager comes from the field, they may think they know everything, including how to do the job, and may still see things from their perspective as things were. This can result in well-intentioned comments such as, "What I did was...," "I'd do this...," or "This is the way to do it," the effect of which can be disempowering. Going back to the floor with the intention to *watch, listen* and *learn* provides the opportunity for a more rounded picture and to gain input from those actually doing the job. After all, they are the ones who know a lot about what could be better – if we choose to involve them and listen to them.

Co-participating as a head teacher

Nigel Gann is an experienced education consultant, and was a head teacher at several tough inner-city schools during his career. He helped us to think through how a head teacher could co-participate during the school day. This list is not just for teachers of course – it contains inspiration for all Host Leaders.

- For a head, co-participating means joining in with the staff, and also the pupils

- Standing outside the school in the mornings, welcoming students and staff – creating an event and a ritual around the beginning of the day

- Smiling, nodding and engaging with people when you see them in the corridor

- Welcoming visitors when they arrive or when they phone for an appointment. If parents or other local stakeholders arrive, they are sent straight in to meet the Head – sales people need an appointment!

- Being at assembly and other events, even if you are not running them or actively participating. Also making sure that these events are inclusive and offer participation for all in various ways

- Participating with the governing body, working with them as a team rather than trying to get ahead. Be prepared to take a problem along and work through it with them, rather than take the problem and the solution you want to apply

- Join in with meals – food and drink breaks and events offer an excellent chance to interact with everyone

- When observing lessons, don't just sit at the back and watch – be prepared sometimes to join in with the lesson and then discuss afterwards

- Don't spend all your time behind a desk! It creates a barrier. Get out and be with people

What would these things look like in *your* situation? Where are the small opportunities for you to co-participate more?

Stepping back

In this chapter, we have explored how the Host Leader is a Co-Participator: he/she organizes things *AND* joins in along with people.

The trick is to balance these two things. The Host Leader doesn't do too much organizing – let's face it; they probably have other people to do some of the organizing. On the other hand, they don't do too much joining in – to the detriment of being aware of what's going on all around them. The balance could be said to come from managing the transitions between phases, between roles, between people.

To manage the transitions, we engage in the dance. In the role of Co-Participator, much of the time the leader is stepped back, with a watching brief, yet always ready to step forward when required. As with any dance, timing makes all the difference. The Co-Participator role is also one of the roles where the leader has the privilege of gallery time, seeing things from many different angles and perspectives. The prize is recognizing things that would otherwise go unnoticed and yet could make all the difference – to people and performance.

Co-Participator

- Look for opportunities to serve others first
- Take a turn with everyday tasks
- Be alert to the "pinch points"

- Step forward to provide, care and support
- Join in and "eat the same food"
- Be prepared to intervene if necessary

Reflective questions

- In what ways can you "serve others first" in your work or workplace?

- What opportunities do you have to take a position alongside everyone else, as a part of the group?

- How might you "eat the same food" as everyone else?

- How might you get "back to the floor" more often to see how things are (as opposed to how they used to be when you were last there)?

- What pinch points can you identify in your organization? How can you be there at the key moments without interfering?

Key points

> Co-participating offers many opportunities to get new perspectives, observe what's happening, and take up different Host Leadership positions.

> Step forward to provide for others first – then join in.

> Step back to take a turn at the everyday tasks – keep your hand in.

> Watch out for pinch points – key moments when you want to be present in the background and ready to step forward.

> Get "back to the floor" occasionally.

12

Using the Six Roles and Four Positions

Are you going to step forward or step back?

That's the question that all hosts have in mind. We have explored the idea of hosting from many angles. We have discussed the six roles of engagement of a Host Leader. We have explored four positions that a Host Leader may take up. So... which of them are speaking to you right now?

In this chapter, we will explore some real situations, showing one way to use these ideas in deciding whether to step forward or back next, how, and in which position. First, let us remind ourselves of the story so far.

Six roles of engagement

Step back	Step forward

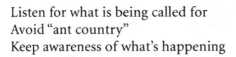

Initiator

Listen for what is being called for	Form a hope, dream or intention
Avoid "ant country"	Get things moving – small steps
Keep awareness of what's happening	Respond with dynamic steering

Inviter

Think about whom to invite
What do you need next?
Offer choice and space for an
authentic Yes

Start with the soft Power of the Ask
Make it personal, attractive,
acknowledging
Extend a welcoming hand

Space Creator

What would be a great space –
physical, interactional and head space?
What message is your space conveying?
Hold the space while people use it

Create a space to support what
you want to happen
Focus on the details as well as the big
picture
Keep the space refreshed, invigorated
and evolving

Gatekeeper

Take note of the thresholds to
your space
Be observant of container size –
could it be changed?
Step back and welcome people from
other boundaries and spaces

Welcome people in and establish
defining routines and rituals
Change container size –
more/fewer people, bigger/smaller
topic
Be prepared to exclude people and
topics – a positive No, temporarily, or
even for the foreseeable future

Connector

Look out for not-yet-connected
people
Look for opportunities to build
connections between others
Be aware of connection all around

Connect with new people and their
"walk" (Level 1)
Connect others – the social butterfly
(Level 2)
Respond to new awareness with
openness – perhaps a new call is
forming? (Level 3)

Co-Participator

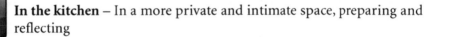

Look for opportunities to serve others first

Take a turn with everyday tasks

Be alert to the "pinch points"

Step forward to provide, care and support

Join in and "eat the same food"

Be prepared to intervene if necessary

And a reminder of our four positions for a host:

In the spotlight – Being the focus of attention, out front, making things happen

 With the guests – Still in view of everyone, but being "one of the group" – not the overall centre of attention

In the gallery – Standing back, taking an overview of what's happening (like Abraham under his tree)

In the kitchen – In a more private and intimate space, preparing and reflecting

Dynamic Steering

Remember the *User's Guide to the Future*. In each case, we will see the host setting a direction, and then using the six roles to decide on some very small next steps. They will then put these into action, and respond and use the subsequent emerging events. This is not about planning the whole journey; it is about having an idea of the destination and then setting out with the first steps.

Dynamic steering means asking, reflecting and reviewing often, looking for progress and then deciding on more next steps – and keeping doing that!

Using the six roles of engagement

The difference between a rule and a role, as we saw at the start of the book, is that, while a rule has to be followed all the time, a role is something we can step in and out of to match the situation. The key questions to ask are therefore:

- **Am I going to step forward or step back (next)?**

- **In which role?**

- **And in which position?**

The following examples will help you to grasp the idea of looking at a situation and thinking about what might be a great next move or two, using this framework:

- Situation – the context and background
- Challenge – hopes/aspirations and key areas of focus
- Roles – which roles seem particularly relevant right now?
- First steps – to put into action right away
- Signs of progress – what happened, and further options

Large organization: Hannah and the coasting team

Situation: Hannah is a newly appointed manager in a team in a large public organization, providing services to the public. She has taken over from someone who had been in the post a long time and has just retired. Hannah has inherited a somewhat dysfunctional and coasting team. There is pressure from above to make improvements – her initial discussions with her boss make it clear that he's not happy with where they are and he needs to see major changes within the next six months with clear signs of progress in three months. The current levels of business are not sufficient to justify offering the service. Specific goals and targets have been set which, if not met, will have significant consequences for the department.

The team consists of a mix of personalities. Jerry and Nick have both been in the team for some time and are very comfortable with the status quo. Claire is dissatisfied with what they are doing and how customers are dealt with but can't see a way forward without more budget (which isn't going to arrive any time soon).

Ian, on the other hand, is a "Young Turk" – ambitious, enthusiastic and full of ideas. He can see lots of ways to change things and gets frustrated that nothing gets done and his colleagues don't want to change. Anna, the team admin support person, plays her role in a calm and organized manner.

Hannah seemed to make some progress with the team in her first couple of weeks but it has tailed off and she is growing increasingly frustrated with the lack of engagement and willingness to change amongst the team.

Challenge: We asked Hannah about her priorities. She said, "How can I engage the team around what is required and how things need to change to create a platform for a sustainable future for us all? We really need to build our customer user base, which will mean engaging all the team members."

Roles: After this conversation, Hannah spent some time thinking about the different roles of engagement. She was immediately struck by needing to find ways to both step back – to get clearer about how things worked here, as a newcomer – without losing the idea of stepping forward to start to exert some influence. The following are the roles she picked up as being particularly important at this point:

Initiator – Listen and notice what's being called for: What is being said? What is not being said? How are the team working together? What are customers saying? Hannah immediately saw a chance to spend time "with the guests;" i.e., with the team, collectively and individually, and with customers too. Even though she has a clear goal, engaging with the team will allow her to ensure that they each understand the situation clearly. Time "in the gallery" will also allow Hannah to observe what's happening. It provides an opportunity to see how the team are interacting, working together and how work flows within the team.

Inviter – Hannah was keen to move on to create a big picture of what the team needs to achieve: a clear six-month "horizon," in the terms of the *User's Guide to the Future*. Hannah wanted to invite the team, as a group, to the big challenge: the hopes, dreams and intentions for the future. This is an "in the spotlight" moment for Hannah as the Host Leader, and provides an opportunity for the team to contribute to the next steps. They can each bring what they think is relevant – things that have worked before as well as new ideas and possibilities. She noted to be careful in making the invitation attractive and acknowledging.

Space Creator – Hannah had been struck by the lack of a good group-meeting space. She decided to step forward and reorganize her space and create a meeting hub with a table and chairs away from the workspace, and invited Anna, the admin support person, to help her.

First steps: Next, Hannah spent time with the team members individually. This gave her a chance to act in the role of:

Connector – Hannah got to know each person individually, connecting with them, finding out what they were good at and what they enjoyed, and listening to their ideas and concerns. This worked particularly well with dissatisfied Claire who, whilst initially unable see a way forward, quickly got engaged. She had been in a similar situation before in a previous job, and saw what she could contribute. Hannah soon recognized that Jerry and Nick both had a lot of experience and knowledge. The key was finding what they enjoyed or especially interested them. Jerry, for example, was very aware of traditions in the team and wanted to carry things forward, things that made the team who they were. Ian was very excited that there was a juicy challenge coming up, and started producing long lists of options … *Maybe too long*, Hannah wondered.

After about a week, the team meeting came around. As she would be "in the spotlight" at the meeting, Hannah again thought about the roles and picked out the following priorities:

Gatekeeper – As new ideas are generated, Hannah will take care not to squash or stifle ideas, initially needing to be inclusive and welcoming of ideas and even inviting others in to contribute from outside the team. Keeping the team focused on the topic of building their customer base will also be important – Hannah was clear that she should be careful not to open the gate too widely to include anything and everything, and should be prepared to park other topics for another day. This was particularly useful with Ian, who had loads of energy and ideas, and just needed to be focused to be more effective.

Co-participator – As a Co-Participator, Hannah is very clear that she is part of the team and is facing the challenge along with everyone else. She will make sure that she puts her ideas and perspectives into the mix along with everyone else, not dominating and yet not pretending she has nothing to contribute. A great opportunity to co-participate is opened up with an early project deadline or milestone. By asking the team what she can do to support them, Hannah can roll up her sleeves and join in.

Signs of progress for Hannah: The meeting was a success, with everyone developing small actions to take things forward. Hannah took on the Initiator role again and helped develop their next "signs of progress" that they would be alert to in the coming week. She also had a role as a "guest" at the management team meeting to share progress and connect Claire with her counterpart in a different department. Essential to this progress is Hannah's ability to create space for herself, the "in the kitchen" space, to review, reflect and plan what's next.

Understanding the importance of dynamic steering will be key to informing Hannah's next steps.

Small business: Laura clears up a mess

Situation: Laura is a newly promoted account director in an advertising agency. As is typical with agency life, there is relatively high staff turnover at all levels, from account exec right up to account director. People tend to work in teams, with each team having account execs, account managers, and headed up by an account director. When an account director or account manager leaves, it is often the case that the next in line steps up to fill the vacancy, creating another vacancy down the line. Managers are promoted with little or no management experience or training – know-how is picked up as they go along and a newly promoted manager may not have been in the agency or indeed in their existing role for long. Life is frenetic: fast-paced, quick turnaround of work to meet deadlines and client expectations, reactive to internal and external demands, with little time for preparation or review from one job to the next.

Laura finds herself in exactly this position: She has been in the agency for about three years, promoted to manager fairly recently, and has now been promoted to director following the departure of the previous incumbent. There is a continuing challenge to recruit and retain account execs, and so her already short-staffed team now has another empty post – which until last week was filled by Laura!

Within the team there are challenges with meeting deadlines. One account manager has already left because of this. There is a real lack of enthusiasm and responsibility across the team. Unless Laura allocates tasks and constantly chases for updates, deadlines are left to slip and be missed. This often means that she has to pick up the tasks herself. Even when she checks in, what she is told can't be relied upon. Client confidence is starting to suffer.

Challenge: Laura is having to pick up too much of the work that should have been done by others. She is at the end of her tether – something has to change or she will be the next to leave. How can she lead the team differently to build some stability and develop their capability to allow them to better serve the needs of their clients?

Roles: When we met with Laura, she was in a mood to step forward! It was time for action. Laura was intrigued by the possibilities offered by the roles of Gatekeeper and Space Creator.

Gatekeeper: Laura saw part of the issue as a lack of focus. There was so much going on that team members lost track of what they were doing for each other, and the result was confusion. In the role of Gate- keeper, a tighter focus could be maintained by closing the gate on some projects – temporarily – to allow clearer priority for others. A smaller container could give large benefits.

Space Creator: Laura's reasoning was that people had gotten accustomed to this mess and chaos, and that it had somehow infected the whole team and their space. The office was a mess of unfinished paperwork, failed pitch materials, unloved ideas and places to lose things amidst the rubble. An invigorated space could give a chance for a fresh look at the work, as well as being a reminder that things had changed and a new phase had started for the team.

Despite their eagerness to get into action, Laura was also aware that she had an opportunity, as a newly appointed account director, to step back and take stock of the situation. She resolved to take a few moments in the gallery every day, to assess how things were going and notice what was being called for next.

First steps: Laura led a swift assault on the office space. She invited everyone in the team to join her in a start-of-day clear-out of everything relating to old projects. All the team accepted, apart from grumpy Ken who had a client offsite meeting. The office immediately took on a newly purposeful appearance. During the clear-out, Laura started a discussion about how she could act more in service and support to the team by ensuring they had what they needed, rather than rushing to patch up what hadn't been done. The team said that, while they were evidently understaffed, a clearer sense of priorities, even on a daily basis, would help. She asked about previously successful projects and then rescued some old posters from the dumpster relating to two of these, to remind the team of their past successes. Ken returned from his meeting amazed to see the office clearer than it had been for years, and joined the discussion about keeping focused.

Laura's Gatekeeping ideas emerged along with the team's desire for some daily information. She started a daily update meeting – maximum fifteen minutes (and timed – if the meeting ran over, everyone put $5 in the charity collection). This ritual in itself began to help all feel more like a team. If any of the team saw that things might go awry (and they would – this is an agency environment after all), they could call on Laura for help. In return, Laura started to gatekeep on new work, closely watching how requirements entered and noting what would be needed by when. Anyone who was asked for the inevitable "Can you just…" request from other units was to refer the request to Laura. She hoped that this would be a temporary feature, which might be relaxed when the vacancies were filled.

Signs of progress: Laura got into the habit of drinking a coffee in the gallery around midmorning while standing in the corner of the office, near the window. The morning meetings were starting to work well. The fifteen minute limit had been breached on the first two days, to some grumbling, but the team had become more effective at keeping the discussion tight. The meeting had also become a place where the team could connect with each other on challenges and needs which were coming up, so that demands didn't just arrive out of the blue.

Laura reflected on the journey she had made from being account manager to director. To start with she had been co-participating too much, picking up work which really should have been done by others. By showing herself in a new light to the team, listening to what was wanted, and putting herself consciously into a serving and support role, she had actually reduced the amount of the everyday work she was picking up. This change in relationship to hosting the team had helped all to reconnect with their work and each other. Their office space was more inviting, they were hitting their deadlines again – and there was $80 in the kitty for the local charity fund. Now it was time to focus on the next challenge – getting a better fix on their customers' needs.

Medium-sized family business: Hosting the boss

Situation: Damian has recently joined a fast-growing engineering manufacturing company as senior operations manager. He brings a wealth of experience from a larger manufacturing company and hopes to bring his expertise on process engineering, operations management and efficiency to bear in his new role.

The success of the business to date is all down to the founding husband and wife team, John and Lisa, who still run the business today. John, the managing director, is a true entrepreneur: innovative, fast, spots opportunities and implements them immediately, aware of everything, and very in-the-moment. He runs the show and everyone looks to him for guidance.

Damian, on the other hand, is used to a very methodical way of working, with Gantt charts, spreadsheets, detailed plans with logical sequencing of events. There are major challenges in the operations area, with contract delays, parts missing from orders, inefficiencies, re-work on jobs. Damian sees what needs to be done and has a clear plan of action, and, whilst John has seemingly agreed with his plans, he keeps picking Damian up on other things he'd like tackled, how he'd like things done differently, why certain things haven't been carried out. John's constant questioning of Damian's approach is driving him to distraction and getting in the way of creating a solid foundation for the next stage of growth for the company.

Challenge: Damian recognizes their different working styles and is keen to find a way to work *with* John rather than what feels like against him. His ideal is that John leave him to get on with the job he has brought him in to do. He is keen to gain John's trust and confidence that operations are in good hands and give him the space to deliver.

Roles: When we introduced Damian to the six roles, he quickly latched on to Initiator, Connector and Gatekeeper.

Initiator – Damian saw the importance of getting some clear horizon hopes and intentions with John. He recognized that John was very talented at spotting new possibilities, and was keen to look for a way to get some clear long-term priorities agreed. The existing issues with production are known to John, who has after all brought Damian in to help him and so presumably knows at some level that he needs a more step-by-step approach. Once they have agreed some clear hopes, there may be a clearer frame for day-to-day operational matters.

Connector – Damian was keen to build his relationship with John and decided that, rather than getting exasperated with John's intuitive approach, he should step back. He wants to find out more about John's "walk" – how he had got to where he was, how the business had started, what successes they had enjoyed so far, and what was key to keep going forward. Perhaps if John knows that Damian knows the story well, he will be able to trust him a little more. Damian also decided to build his connections with others in the business on a general basis.

Gatekeeper – Damian saw great possibilities in keeping a close eye on the container size of his conversations with John. Keeping a focus on the operations activities could be achieved by temporarily closing the gate on other topics and smart use of a positive No. Perhaps an occasional more wide-ranging conversation could be scheduled. Damian was very keen to show progress on the key issues, and keep those in the foreground.

Signs of progress: Damian met with John and had a very productive discussion about the horizon. Together they developed a shared view of key issues, which they call the "Vital Few." Damian saw how well John responded to news of progress in this direction, and is learning to keep his detailed plans as his own working documents. He uses these to keep an eye on small next steps coming up and to be prepared for the unexpected.

John was delighted to introduce Damian to the history of the business, and they now share both the story and the language of past events, successes and disappointments. Damian is learning how John's strengths have developed the business to its current situation, and can see more clearly how his own different perspective can help bring new dimensions without interfering with what has helped John to succeed so far. Indeed, John is becoming more and more pleased that he doesn't have to spend time chasing details of production hiccups and can spend more time meeting customers and innovating. He likes the focus of his meetings with Damian, and can spend more time co-participating with other teams.

Community organization: Turning around a dwindling group

Situation: George is chair of Live Better, a community organization based in a university town in the USA. Live Better works to bring people together in an inclusive way, to support each other, help people make personal connections in a busy urban environment, and gather volunteers to work on community action projects such as making food at centers for the homeless and maintaining play areas for children.

George has a small team of dedicated helpers, and together they put on a monthly meeting. These meetings are great fun – a mixture of listening to talks, singing together, moments of reflection and coffee and cake afterwards. This group has been running for around eighteen months, and after an enthusiastic start, the monthly participation has leveled out at around a hundred, of which around twenty are consistently getting involved in the community work. During the past few months, however, George has noticed a drop-off in attendance and his helpers don't seem as fired up as they once were.

George is concerned that the group is losing momentum. He has noticed that, while many of the participants are getting on very well, they also seem to not be as welcoming to newcomers as was once the case. While forming a community spirit is central to Live Better's work, he worries that a lack of new participants will start to lead to a dwindling group. He is feeling the need for a call to action to do something about this.

Challenge: George is concerned that the group is becoming a little cliquey. He needs to work on bringing in new members, making them welcome, and showing the work of Live Better on a broader stage in the city.

Roles: After George had read through the six roles' descriptions, the ones which jumped out at him were Gatekeeper, Inviter and Connector.

Gatekeeper – George is in a good position to open the gate wider: he can boundary-span. By looking for other communities to meet, George can take the word about Live Better to whole groups of people rather than simply individuals. George can step forward in his capacity as chair to represent the group on a wider basis with similar-but-different groups. As this is a college town, the university could prove very fruitful. George can also reach out to groups which may include both potential participants and potential recipients of community action. He may wish to take some time in the kitchen with his helper team to prepare for this, to compare notes on possibilities and to invite them to join his initiative.

Inviter – George can look for opportunities to offer some compelling invitations as he goes about spanning boundaries. The Live Better meetings are always fun and energizing, so he has an interesting offer to make. George will be aware that invitations are about soft power and choice, so he will be careful not to overstep the mark in his enthusiasm to get people to come along. And of course, when people take up his invitations, he will notice their arrival and be there to welcome them in. Which brings us to:

Connector – As well as building connections with the new people (level 1), George will be on the lookout for opportunities to make connections between people (level 2). He will be alert to connecting those with things to offer to the community – skills, resources, contacts, time – with those in need of these things. George decides to extend possibilities for connections outside the monthly meetings, and engages his team in helping to organize a series of potluck suppers, providing the opportunity for more relaxed connection in a social environment.

First steps: George took some time in the kitchen to think about groups to engage. He had noticed that a transition group was meeting in a local pub and decided to go along to introduce himself, see what they were focusing on and how there might be some common goals and synergy.

He also decided to focus on improving the welcome for new participants, both by making some better signs to show newcomers to the hall and by being there by the door in person to look out for new faces and say hello. George also resolved to find some time in the gallery during the next meeting, to see better for himself how things were going, how people were interacting and if anyone was being left out. He was keen to see how much his perception of cliques was borne out in reality.

Finally, George made a note to raise these issues with his team of helpers, and engage them in the idea of some different ways to connect outside the usual meetings.

Signs of progress: George took the spotlight to share his thoughts with his team at their regular meeting. It transpired that Carrie, the group's treasurer, had a neighbor who was involved with a food-bank scheme in the downtown area. Another committee member had contacts in the university's business school, who were always looking out for interesting projects for students to get involved with.

At the next meeting, George and Carrie positioned themselves carefully near the entrance to be with the guests, and managed to say hello to over a dozen first-time participants. One group of four students was particularly interested in community environmental action, and George made sure to guide them towards Alex, the community action coordinator, who was working on helping a recycling project. The students commented on how welcoming they found George's new signs.

Taking a moment in the gallery at the end of the meeting, George noticed that most of the newcomers had stayed for a coffee and looked to be enjoying themselves with some of the regulars. He also noticed that the table at the back where people could sign up for activities (including the potluck dinners) looked a bit bare and unattractive, and started to think about how the meeting space might be gingered up for next month …

So what's *YOUR* situation right now?

These examples reflect some of the myriad scenarios we've heard from people along our journey to date with Host Leadership. As we have introduced people to the metaphor and shared the six roles and four positions with them, we have asked them these very same questions:

- **Are you going to step forward or step back (next)?**

- **In which role?**

- **And in which position?**

In each encounter, the leader's thinking has shifted and in turn new possibilities have opened up.

As you've come along this journey with us, we are sure your own leadership opportunities and challenges have surfaced. Hopefully you've already identified some next steps that are bringing about change.

As you continue to regularly step back and listen to what is being called for, we invite you to become part of the Host Leadership movement by joining the Host Leadership community at www.hostleadership.com. Here you can find useful resources, share your own Host Leadership stories, contribute to the conversation and support others on their Host Leadership journey. We look forward to welcoming you there.

13

Open Your Heart – Then Open the Door

"If there is room in the heart, there is room in the house."

~ Danish proverb

We have come a long way since the start of this book – the metaphor of the host, the host/guest relationship at the heart of this work, the flexibility of roles (not rules). We have examined what hosts do now, what they have done through the ages, and around the world in different cultures and societies. Hosting is at the centre of humanity, and a little more awareness of the value of reaching out and opening our doors will go a long way to building relationship in teams, organizations, communities and movements.

A lifelong journey

We hope that you, the reader, are now more skilled, more confident and more aware in your hosting practice. Well done! Opening our eyes to the ways that hosting works is a vital step along this road. In the words of Art of Hosting network member Jerry Nagel, "Becoming a good host is not easy, takes practice, and is a lifelong learning journey."

Part of this journey is continually developing our awareness of the subtleties of working with people in space. Some people call this the "energy" of the space. Mark, as a recovering physicist, prefers to use that word in its scientific context. However, he is the first to agree that when an experienced host steps into a space filled with people, there is something that comes across about how things are and which way things may move. Working with this awareness, taking steps to hold the space and move it in a useful direction, are the next steps of development for the budding Host Leader.

The profound and the mundane

You may have noticed that this book has not spoken a great deal about the "big questions" of humanity – love, understanding, fear, purpose, family, enlightenment. This is not because we view these as unimportant – far from it. However, we think that the way into these big things is through the small things – the details, the tiny signs that show something, the almost imperceptible responses we give to others when we meet them.

It's one thing to talk grandly about the importance of love, respect and empowerment. It is quite another to be able to *do* these things, in tiny detail, in human interaction. One of our colleagues, very keen on post-heroic leadership, has a way of forcefully exclaiming, "It's not about me!" to emphasize his point. Every time we meet him, he seems to be having another loud attempt to convince people that "it's not about me!" – apparently oblivious to the point that while he keeps talking loudly, forcefully and continuously, it is *ALL* about him.

Learning to open your heart

We think that developing as a host means one thing above all – learning to open our hearts. Imagine being at home on a stormy night, when the doorbell rings. It is a bedraggled stranger. They have nothing, and seek shelter. What do we do? Threaten to call the police? Give them some money to go away? Or invite them in? This is a question for each of us, and there is no easy answer.

This is a question for us all. We can start in small ways. Look around. Make eye contact. Help strangers when the opportunity comes along. Listen to their "walk." Reach out with the soft power of invitation. And then reflect; talk to others about the experience. The difference between connection and no connection can be the blink of an eye, the stretching out of a hand, a word of interest. In the words of seventeenth-century writer John Bunyan:

> "*You haven't lived today until you've done something for someone who can never repay you.*"

Now start again

This book contains a wide range of stories, traditions, ideas, and metaphors to help us think about hosting as leadership. One way to continue your journey would be to turn right back to the beginning and start again. The Greek philosopher Heraclitus famously said that it's impossible to step into the same river twice. The full quote comes in two parts[1] and can be summed up as "*No man ever steps in the same river twice, for it's not the same river and he's not the same man.*" In the same way, you are not the same person as the one who started reading this book, and your understanding (and therefore the book) has moved on in the meantime. You can't read the same book twice.

So, go back to the start and begin again. This time, the stories and metaphors will speak to you in a different way. You will be more clued in to the possibilities, more aware of the subtleties, and in a better position to think again about your hosting and leadership.

The host is both the first and the last

When you go back to the start, you will see that we began with this quotation:

> "*The host is both the first and the last.*"
>
> ~Old Arabic proverb

This is a good example of the profound and the mundane. The host is physically there first as they have to prepare the space and get ready to welcome their guests. They are also the last as they have to clear up and turn off the lights.

However, take another look. The host is the first – it starts with me. If I do not have an open door, a warm welcome and an open heart, then nothing will happen. Of course I will engage others, we will quickly build things together, the future will emerge, for better or worse.

The host is also the last – the one who will put themselves last, the one who may not be noticed in the excitement and wonder at what is developing, the one who knows when to step back. This is beautifully captured in this poem, a translation of the Tao Te Ching 34 by Witter Bynner:[2]

> *"Bountiful life, letting anyone attend,*
> *Making no distinction between left or right.*
> *Feeding everyone, refusing no one,*
> *Has not provided this bounty to show how much it owns,*
> *Has not fed and clad its guests with any thought of claim;*
> *And because it lacks the twist*
> *Of mind or body in what it has done,*
> *The guile of head or hands,*
> *Is not always respected by a guest.*
> *Others appreciate welcome from the perfect host*
> *Who, barely appearing to exist,*
> *Exists the most."*

Further reading and materials

You can access free bonus materials and resources at www.hostleadership.com. Simply go to

www.hostleadership.com/bonus/

and sign in using the code HOST17.

Want to explore more about the ideas in *Host*? Join one of our interactive online classes—you'll be able to get familiar with the ideas, apply them in your own work, ask questions, interact with your classmates, and join the worldwide Host Leadership community.

Want to introduce your organization to Host Leadership? Contact us via the website to set up keynote speeches, executive briefings and engaging workshops.

Connect with us on Twitter @thehostleader, #hostleadership

Notes

Chapter 1

1. Purcell, J., Kinnie, N., Hutchinson, S., Rayton, B. and Swart, J. (2003). Understanding the People and Performance Link: Unlocking the black box. London, CIPD.
2. Grint, K. (2010). Leadership: A very short introduction. Oxford: Oxford University Press.
3. Bob Johansen interview in Forum, 2010, Speed in a VUCA World: How leaders of the future will execute strategy http://www.forum.com/downloads/transcripts/VUCA-Interview-2010-Final.pdf.
4. Organizations & People, Volume 20 No 3 (Autumn 2013) – special issue on leadership paradoxes.
5. Binney, G., Wilke, G., and Williams, C. (2009) Living Leadership: A practical guide for ordinary heroes, 2nd Edition, London: Pearson Financial Times.
6. Johansen ibid.
7. McKergow, M., W., (2009). Leader as Host, Host as Leader: Towards a new yet ancient metaphor. International Journal for Leadership in Public Services Vol 5 No 1 pp. 19–24.
8. Jan Gunnarsson and Olle Blohm. From Boss To Host: The Art of Welcoming Leadership, Värdskepet Utveckling (2011).
9. Deborah Frieze and Margaret Wheatley, From Hero to Host: A Story of Citizenship in Columbus, Ohio, Berkana Institute, (2011), retrieved from http://www.berkana.org/pdf/FromHerotoHost_web.pdf.
10. Bennis, W. in the introduction to Parks, S.D. (2005) Leadership Can Be Taught: A bold approach for a complex world, Boston: Harvard Business School Press p. xi–xii.
11. George Bizos's interview with John Carlin, retrieved from http://www.pbs.org/wgbh/pages/frontline/shows/mandela/interviews/bizos.html.

Chapter 2

1. Tim Cope interviewed on BBC Radio 4 program Saturday Live, 30 November 2013.
2. Genesis Chapter 18 verses 2-8.
3. Sharon Daloz Parks. (2005). Leadership Can Be Taught: A Bold Approach for a Complex World, Harvard Business School Press, 2005, p. 201.
4. William B Joiner and Stephen A Josephs. (2006), Leadership Agility: Five Levels of Mastery for Anticipating and Initiating Change. Jossey Bass.
5. Lone Hersted and Kenneth Gergen (2013), Releational Leading, Taos Institute Publications.

6. Rule of St Benedict retrieved from http://www.ccel.org/ccel/benedict/rule2/files /rule2.html – The rule is available in various versions and translations.
7. Joseph M. Marshall III. (2001). *The Lakota Way: Stories and Lessons For Living.* New York: Viking Compass, quotes from p. 12 and p. 19.

Chapter 3

1. Pollington, Stephen. (2003). *The Mead Hall: The Feasting Tradition in Anglo-Saxon England.* Hockwold-cum-Wilton: Anglo-Saxon Books.
2. Sinek, Simon. (2014). *Leaders Eat Last: Why Some Teams Pull Together and Others Don't.* Portfolio.

Chapter 4

1. Stewart, Ian and Cohen, Jack (1999). *Figments of Reality: The evolution of the curious mind.* Cambridge UK: Cambridge University Press.
2. Some readers will know that the idea of continuous steering is present in cybernetics, which itself comes from the Greek word *kybernetes* or steersman.
3. Jackson, Paul Z and McKergow, Mark. (2007). The Solutions Focus: Making coaching & change SIMPLE. London: Nicholas Brealey Publishing, Art Tatum story on p. 105.

Chapter 5

1. John J Oliver (2001), *The Team Enterprise Solution*, Oak Tree Press.
2. Ronald A Heifetz, (1994). *Leadership Without Easy Answers.* , Cambridge MA: Harvard University Press.
3. Simon Walker. (2007). *The Undefended Leader Trilogy, Volumes 1 and 2, Leading Out of Who You are & Leading With Nothing to Lose.* Piquant.
4. Stephen R. Covey. (1990). *The 7 Habits of Highly Effective People.* Free Press.

Chapter 6

1. Joseph Campbell, quoted Nelson, Thorana. (ed.) (2010). *Doing Something Different: Solution-focused brief therapy practices.* New York: Routledge p. 278.
2. Campbell, Joseph. (1949). *The Hero with a Thousand Faces.* New World Library (Republished 2012).
3. Jackson, Paul Z and McKergow, Mark. (2002). *The Solutions Focus: The SIMPLE Way to Positive Change.* London: Nicholas Brealey Publishing. Mark has published two other SF books, *Positive Approaches to Change* and *Solutions Focus Working.*
4. Live Aid 1985; A day of magic. CNN, retrieved from http://edition.cnn.com/2005 /SHOWBIZ/Music/07/01/liveaid.memories/index.html.
5. Geldof, Bob. (1986) *Is That It?* Penguin Books.
6. Suzuki, Shunryu. (2011). *Zen Mind, Beginner's Mind.* Shambhala Press.

Chapter 7

1. Joseph Nye (2008). *The Powers To Lead*. Oxford University Press p. 30.
2. Jeff Immelt, quoted in Nye, J. (2010). Power and Leadership. In NOHRIA, N., & KHURANA, R. (eds.), Handbook of leadership theory and practice. A Harvard Business School centennial colloquium. Harvard Business Press, pp. 305–332. Quote on p. 317.
3. Adapted from John Carlin, Playing The Enemy, Atlantic Books 2008 pp 154–155.
4. Ralph Stacey (2005). Experiencing Emergence in Organizations: Local Interaction and the Emergence of Global Patterns (Complexity as the Experience of Organizing). London: Routledge.
5. Paul Z Jackson and Mark McKergow (2007). The Solutions Focus: Making coaching and change SIMPLE. London: Nicholas Brealey Publishing.
6. "When we don't use the 'Power of the Ask,' we are in essence saying '*no*' before the question has even been asked." Deborah Mills-Scofield, Harvard Business Review Blog (2013) http://blogs.hbr.org/cs/2013/01/the_power_of_your_network_is_t.html.
7. Lord Rees quoted in the Telegraph, 19 May 2014, http://www.telegraph.co.uk/science/science-news/10841125/Calling-all-geniuses-for-the-new-Longitude-Prize.html.
8. Joseph Nye (2008). Ibid *The Powers to Lead* p. 148.

Chapter 8

1. The concept of *Ba* – see, for example Kitaro Nishida. (1990). *An inquiry into the Good* (translated by M Abe and C Ives) New Haven, CT: Yale University Press, and Ikujiro Nonaka and Noboru Konno. (1998). The concept of *Ba*: Building foundation for Knowledge Creation. California Management Review Vol 40, No.3 Spring 1998.
2. J.F.O. MCALLISTER. (1999). The Deal Is Done By Belfast Time Magazine, Monday, Dec. 06, 1999 http://content.time.com/time/world/article/0,8599,2050206,00.html.
3. These ideas inspired by Jerry Nagel, Art of Hosting network, in a posting to the AoH listserv May 2014.
4. Jackson, Paul Z and McKergow, Mark. (2002). The Solutions Focus: The SIMPLE Way to Positive Change. London: Nicholas Brealey Publishing.
5. Philip Newman-Hall, Interview with Mark McKergow, 26 July 2012.
6. Harry Murray interview with Mark McKergow, 21 August 2012.
7. Denise Wright personal email to Mark McKergow.
8. Neil Usher, interview with Mark McKergow, 1 February 2013.

Chapter 9

1. Pohl, Christine D. (1999). *Making Room: Recovering hospitality as a Christian tradition*. Grand Rapids MI: Eerdmans, Christine Pohl, Making Room 94-95.
2. Stacey, Ralph. (2007). *Strategic Management and Organisational Dynamics: The Challenge of Complexity to Ways of Thinking about Organisations*. Pearson Education p. 285.

3. Godin, Seth. (2008). *Tribes: We need you to lead us.* London: Piatkus.
4. Olson, Edward E, and Eoyang, Glenda H. (2001). *Facilitating Organisational Change: Lessons from Complexity.* Jossey-Bass/Pfeiffer.
5. Richard Millington (2012). *Buzzing Communities.* London: Feverbee.
6. Ernst, Chris and Chrobot-Mason, Donna. (2010). *Boundary Spanning Leadership: Six Practices for Solving Problems, Driving Innovation, and Transforming Organizations .* McGraw-Hill Professional.
7. Carlin, John (2008). *Playing The Enemy: Nelson Mandela and the Game that made a nation.* Penguin.
8. Rittenberg, Sidney. (1993). *The Man Who Stayed Behind.* Simon and Schuster.
9. Quinn, Ian. (2012). Tesco sends nearly 5,000 managers back to the shop floor – The Grocer, 21 December 2012, retrieved from http://www.thegrocer.co.uk/companies/supermarkets/tesco/tesco-sends-nearly-5000-managers-back-to-the-shop-floor/235130.article.
10. Ury, William. (2008). *The power of a Positive No.* Hodder.
11. Example of a positive No from our colleague Shakya Kumara, retrieved from http://www.briefmindfulness.com/positive-no/.

Chapter 10

1. Bennis, W. in the introduction to Parks, S.D. (2005) Leadership Can Be Taught: A bold approach for a complex world, Boston: Harvard Business School Press p. xi–xii.
2. Wilson, Emily. (2001). The Guardian, 16 May 2001, retrieved from http://www.theguardian.com/education/2001/may/16/universityguide.emilywilson.
3. Jill Pearman, interview with Mark McKergow, Sydney, 4 June 2012. Thanks to Jason Pascoe for setting it up.
4. Fredrickson, Barbara. (2009). *Positivity: Groundbreaking Research Reveals How to Embrace the Hidden Strength of Positive Emotions, Overcome Negativity, and Thrive.* Crown Publishing Group.
5. Jaworski, Joseph. (2011). *Synchronicity: The Inner Path of Leadership* 2nd edition Berrett-Koehler p. 59.
6. Sproat, G. M. (1990). Quoted in Douglas Cole and Ira Chaikin, *An Iron Hand upon the People: The Law against the Potlatch on the Northwest Coast* (Vancouver and Toronto 1990), p. 15.
7. Bynner, Witter. (1988). *The Way of Life According to Lao Tzu.* New York: Penguin Putnam.

Chapter 11

1. Henri JM Nouwen (1976), Reaching Out: The Three Movements of the Spiritual Life, London: William Collins Sons & Co Ltd.
2. The Problem of Executive Isolation, Ron Ashkenas, Harvard Blog Network retrieved from http://blogs.hbr.org/2013/07/why-we-isolate-senior-leaders/.
3. The Kitchen at the Golden Temple Feeds up to 100,000 People a Day for Free. Retrieved from http://twistedsifter.com/2012/08/kitchen-at-the-golden-temple-feeds-people-for-free-langar/.

4. Serve To Lead, IndieBooks (2013).
5. H Jones VC citation, online at http://www.historylearningsite.co.uk/h_jones.htm.
6. Harry Murray, interview with Mark McKergow, 1 August 2012.

Chapter 13

1. Heraclitus, as quoted in Plato's Cratylus 401d and 402a.
2. Bynner, Witter. (1988). *The Way of Life According to Lao Tzu*. New York: Penguin Putnam.

Acknowledgements

We would like to thank the following for their time and expertise in engaging with and discussing Host Leadership with us:

The first in this list is Dr Matthias Varga von Kibèd, whose mentioning of the old Arabic proverb, "The host is both the first and the last," sparked this decade of work and research and set the project on track. This call to action has proved irresistible to us.

Barnet Bain was invaluable in helping us see the wood for the trees and bringing out key messages we had seen and yet not seen. Step forward, Barnet.

Stephen Josephs has inspired our interest in Eastern thinking and has supported this work over many years, as well as contributing a Foreword, and singing and playing guitar.

Ivan and Beth Misner have been great supporters along this road – thank you for so many connections and delightful times.

We have interviewed many leaders and hosts, and are very grateful for their time and insights. Thanks to Sir Chris Bonington, Harry Murray (Lucknam Park), Philip Newman-Hall (Le Manoir aux Quat'Saisons), Bob Davies, Neil Usher, Simon Walker (The Leadership Community), Jerry Nagel (the Art of Hosting network), William Ury, Jill Pearman, Garry Creighton, Kanat Wano, Nigel Gann, Phil Aspden, Denise Wright, Debbie and Dave Hogan, Fred Psyk, Mike Brent, Doug Hennessy, Steve Onyett, Shakya Kumara.

Many of Mark's colleagues in the Transformational Leadership Council came forward with reflections and ideas. Many thanks to Lynne Twist, Stewart and Joanie Emery, Paul Scheele, Raymond Aaron, Martin Rutte, Pete Bissonette, Jim Selman, Sam Horn, Guy Stickney, Dierdre Hade, Terry Tillman, Jeddah Mali, Ray Blanchard, Veronica and Florencia de Andres, Gabriel Nossovitch, Scott Coady, Jim Selman, Cherie Clark, Donna Steinhorn, Robert Richman, Robert MacPhee and Marcia Martin.

Many people have helped us along the way with making connections, setting up meetings, engaging others, joining in with exploratory discussions and being interested enough to make contributions. Thank you to Kat Astley, Penny West, Stuart Rimmer, John Campbell, Jason Pascoe, Craig Sked, Sarah Anthony, Leah Davcheva, David Rose, Sanderson Jones, Pippa Evans, Bob Marshall, Elaine Mosimann, Maria Jicheva, Trevor Durnford, Malin Morén, Paul Wicks and Paul Thistlethwaite.

To all the people who have already openly welcomed the ideas in this book and immediately applied them in their work, thank you for your part in shaping the ideas.

Our thanks to all those who have joined and participated in the Host Leadership online community at www.hostleadership.com. You have given initial momentum and support to this new paradigm.

Oriana Ascanio was our long-suffering and enormously helpful and patient writing coach through the difficult period of bringing the book together. Thank you, Oriana – you are somehow in here with us. Sharon and Jason at Beech Tree Cottages provided a great writing environment at various stages.

Our thanks to the hard-working people who set aside time to read drafts and make very useful suggestions: Stuart Rimmer, John Brooker, Alan Lyons, John Wheeler, Peter Sundman, and Paul Wicks (again!).

Our thanks go to Miles Bailey and the team at Action Publishing Technology for their customary expertise and efficiency. Debbie Brunettin took on the task of translating the book into American English.

From Helen, heartfelt thanks to Jack for being mindful of creating and allowing the space for me to work on this project, and to Lucy for your wise comments and for continuing to shine. So grateful to you both for your gifts. And, finally, to Mark, for inviting me to co-participate, a huge thank you.

Mark would like to thank Jenny Clarke, always his first and sternest editor, for absolutely everything over more than two decades. Without you, Jenny, none of this would have been the same.

About the authors

Dr Mark McKergow is an international speaker, consultant and teacher. A "recovering physicist," his work over more than two decades has focused on responsive and emergent approaches to complex situations. Mark has developed and hosted many aspects of the international Solutions Focus (SF) community since 2000, and is co-author of three related books including bestseller *The Solutions Focus*. He has been closely involved with founding both the SOLWorld network and the SFCT professional body for SF consultants and trainers. He edits the SFCT peer-reviewed journal *InterAction* and is a member of the Transformational Leadership Council. Mark is also a visiting research fellow in philosophy of psychology at the University of Hertfordshire, where he is investigating embodied and narrative paradigms of psychology and change. He lives in London.

Helen Bailey is Managing Director and Head of Coaching at coaching and change company PINNA Ltd. Helen comes from a successful career as a senior manager with The Royal Bank of Scotland Group. She pursued her interest in performance improvement through coaching, undertaking a coaching qualification, and now works with a wide range of organizations in the public and private sectors, facilitating coaching and leadership development programs for coaching directors and managers. Helen works collaboratively with clients to understand their challenges and identify and implement solutions to bring about change. 2010 saw Helen complete the next stage of her own personal development, achieving a distinction in a Master's degree in Developing Professional Practice, for which her research interest was collaboration. She lives in England's Lake District.

Bibliography

This bibliography includes books and other writings we have enjoyed and that inspired us in many ways, as well as book cited in the text.

George Binney, Gerhard Wilke, and Colin Williams (2009), *Living Leadership: A practical guide for ordinary heroes*, 2nd Edition, London: Pearson Financial Times.

Richard Boyatzis and Annie McKee (2005), *Resonant Leadership*, Boston MA: Harvard Business School Press

Witter Bynner (1988), *The Way of Life According to Lao Tzu*, New York: Penguin Putnam

Joseph Campbell (1949), *The Hero with a Thousand Faces*, New World Library (Republished 2012)

John Carlin (2008), *Playing The Enemy: Nelson Mandela and the Game that made a nation*, Penguin

Joan Chittister OSB (1991), *Wisdom Distilled From The Daily: Living the rule of St Benedict today*, New York: HarperSanFrancisco

Joan Chittister OSB (2000), *Illuminated Life: Monastic wisdom for seekers of light*, Mayknoll NY: Orbis Books (2000)

Tim Cope (2013), *On the Trail of Genghis Khan*, London: Bloomsbury Publishing

Chris Corrigan (2010), Reflections on Invitation *http://chriscorrigan.com/parkinglot/ (2010)*

Stephen R. Covey (1990), *The Seven Habits of Highly Effective People*, Free Press

Stephen Denning (2007), *The Secret Language of Leadership: How leaders inspire action through narrative*, San Francisco: Jossey Bass

Max DePree (1992), *Leadership Jazz*, New York: Dell Publishing

Chris Ernst and Donna Chrobot-Mason (2010), *Boundary Spanning Leadership: Six Practices for Solving Problems, Driving Innovation, and Transforming Organizations*, McGraw-Hill Professional

Barbara Fredrickson (2009), *Positivity: Groundbreaking Research Reveals How to Embrace the Hidden Strength of Positive Emotions, Overcome Negativity, and Thrive*, Crown Publishing Group

Deborah Frieze and Margaret Wheatley (2011), *From Hero to Host: A Story of Citizenship in Columbus, Ohio*, Berkana Institute, retrieved from http://www.berkana.org/pdf/FromHerotoHost_web.pdf

Timothy Fry (ed), *The Rule of St Benedict*, Collegeville MI: The Liturgical Press (1982)

Howard Gardner (1995), *Leading Minds: An anatomy of leadership*, London: HarperCollins

Bob Geldof (1986), *Is That It?*, Penguin Books

Seth Godin (2008), *Tribes: We need you to lead us*, London: Piatkus

Robert K Greenleaf (1977), *Servant Leadership*, New York: Paulist Press

Robert K Greenleaf (1991), *The Servant as Leader*, Robert K Greenleaf Center

Keith Grint (2010), *Leadership: A very short introduction*, Oxford: Oxford University Press.

Jan Gunnarsson and Olle Blohm (2008), *Hostmanship: The Art of Making People Feel Welcome*, Dialogos Förlag

Jan Gunnarsson and Olle Blohm (2011). *From Boss To Host: The Art of Welcoming Leadership*, Värdskepet Utveckling

Leslie A Hay (2006), *Hospitality: The heart of spiritual direction*, New York: Morehouse Publishing

John Heider (1986), *The Tao of Leadership*, Aldershot: Wildwood House

Ronald A Heifitz (1994), *Leadership Without Easy Answers*, Cambridge MA: Harvard University Press

Ronald A Heifitz and Marty Linsky (2002), *Leadership On The Line: Staying alive through the dangers of leadership*, Cambridge MA: Harvard University Press

Lone Hersted and Kenneth Gergen (2013), *Relational Leading*, Taos Institute Publications

Herman Hesse (1956, republished 1992), *The Journey To The East*, New York: The Noonday Press

Fr Daniel Homan OSB and Lonni Collins Pratt (2005), *Radical Hospitality: Benedict's way of love*, Brewster MA: Paraclete Press

Paul Z Jackson and Mark McKergow (2007), *The Solutions Focus: Making coaching & change SIMPLE*, 2nd edition, London: Nicholas Brealey Publishing

Joseph Jaworski (2011), *Synchronicity: The Inner Path of Leadership*, 2nd edition, Berrett-Koehler

Bill Joiner and Stephen Josephs (2007), *Leadership Agility*, San Francisco: Jossey Bass

Stephen Josephs (2013), *Dragons at Work*, Tao Alchemical Press

John Koenig (2001), *New Testament Hospitality: Partnership with strangers as promise and mission*, Eugene OR: Wipf and Stock

Georg von Krogh, Kazuo Ichijo and Ikujiro Nonaka (2000), *Enabling Knowledge Creation*, Oxford: Oxford Univerity Press

Satish Kumar (2002), *You Are Therefore I Am: A declaration of dependence*, Dartington: Green Books Ltd

George Lakoff and Mark Johson (1999), *Philosophy in the Flesh: The embodied mind and its challenge to western thought*, New York: Basic Books

Conrad Lashley and Alison Morrison (eds) (2000), *In Search of Hospitality: Theoretical Perspective and Debates*, Oxford: Butterworth-Heinemann

David MacLeod and Nita Clarke (2009), *Engaging for Success: Enhancing employee performance through engagement*, London: Department for Business, Innovation and Skills

Sheila Macnamee and Kenneth J Gergan (eds) (1999), *Relational Responsibility: Resources for Sustainable Dialogue*, London: SAGE Publications

Joanna Macy (1991), *The Dharma of Natural Systems: Mutual Causality and Buddhism and General Systems Theory*, Albany NY: State University of New York

Joseph M. Marshall III (2001), *The Lakota Way: Stories and Lessons For Living*, New York: Viking Compass

Mark McKergow (2009), Leader as Host, Host as Leader: Towards a new yet ancient metaphor, *International Journal for Leadership in Public Services* Vol 5 No 1 pp. 19-24

Anthony de Mello (1990), *Awareness*, London: Fount Paperbacks

Thorana Nelson (ed) (2010), *Doing Something Different: Solution-focused brief therapy practices*, New York: Routledge

Elizabeth Newman (2007), *Untamed Hospitality: Welcoming God and other strangers*, Grand Rapids, MI: Brazos Press

Kitaro Nishida (1990), *An inquiry into the Good*, translated by M Abe and C Ives (New Haven, CT: Yale University Press

Ikujiro Nonaka and Noboru Konno (1998), The concept of "Ba': Building foundation for Knowledge Creation, *California Management Review* Vol 40, No.3

Ikujiro Nonaka and Hirotaka Tekeuchi (1995), *The Knowledge-Creating Company*, Oxford:Oxford University Press

Henri JM Nouwen (1976), *Reaching Out: The Three Movements of the Spiritual Life*, London: William Collins Sons & Co Ltd

Joseph Nye Jr (2008), *The Powers To Lead*, Oxford: Oxford University Press

John J Oliver (2001), *The Team Enterprise Solution*, Oak Tree Press

Edward E Olson and Glenda Eoyang (2001), *Facilitating Organisational Change: Lessons from Complexity,* Jossey-Bass/Pfeiffer

Sharon Daloz Parks (2005), *Leadership Can Be Taught: A bold approach for a complex world*, Boston: Harvard Business School Press

Christine D Pohl (1999), *Making Room: Recovering hospitality as a Christian tradition*, Grand Rapids MI: Eerdmans

Stephen Pollington (2003), *The Mead Hall: The Feasting Tradition in Anglo-Saxon England*, Hockwold-cum-Wilton: Anglo-Saxon Book

John Purcell, Nicholas Kinnie, Sue Hutchinson, Bruce Rayton and Juani Swart (2003), *Understanding the People and Performance Link: Unlocking the black box*, London: CIPD

Radha (Dennis Rose) (1991), *The Zen Way to be an Effective Manager*, London: Mercury Books

Sidney Rittenberg (1993), *The Man Who Stayed Behind*, Simon and Schuster

David Rock (2006), *Quiet Leadership*, New York: Collins

Sandhurst Royal Military Academy (2013) *Serve To Lead*, IndieBooks

Marjorie Schiller, Bea Mah Holland, and Deanna Riley (eds) (2001), *Appreciative Leaders: In the eye of the beholder*, Taos NM: Taos Institute

Peter Senge, C Otto Scharmer, Joseph Jaworski, and Betty Sue Flowers (2005), *Presence: Exploring profound change in people, organizations and society*, London: Nicholas Brealey Publishing

Simon Sinek (2014), *Leaders Eat Last: Why Some Teams Pull Together and Others Don't*, Portfolio.

Larry C Spears (ed) (1995), *Reflections on Leadership: How Robert K Greenleaf's theory of servant-leadership influenced today's top management thinkers*, New York: John Wiley and Sons

Ralph Stacey (2001), *Complex Responsive Processes in Organizations: Learning and Knowledge Creation*, London: Routledge

Ralph Stacey (2005), *Experiencing Emergence in Organizations: Local Interaction and the Emergence of Global Patterns (Complexity as the Experience of Organizing)*, London: Routledge

Ralph Stacey (2007), *Strategic Management and Organisational Dynamics: The Challenge of Complexity to Ways of Thinking about Organisations*, Pearson Education

Ian Stewart and Jack Cohen (1999), *Figments of Reality: The evolution of the curious mind*, Cambridge UK: Cambridge University Press

Arthur Sutherland (2006), *I Was A Stranger: A Christian Theology of Hospitality*, Nashville TN: Abingdon Press

Shunryu Suzuki (1970), *Zen Mind, Beginner's Mind*, Boston: Weatherhill

Thich Nhat Hanh (1997), *Interbeing*, Delhi: Inner Circle

Jane Tomaine (2005), St Benedict's Toolbox: The nuts and bolts of everyday Benedictine living, Harrisburg PA: Morehouse Publishing

William Ury (2008), *The power of a Positive No*, Hodder

Simon Walker (2005), *Subversive Leadership*, Oxford: leadershipcommunity

Simon Walker (2007), *Leading Out of Who You Are: Discovering the Secret of Undefended Leadership*, Piquant Editions

Simon Walker (2007), *Leading with Nothing to Lose: Training in the Excercise of Power: Undefended Leader Part 2*, Piquant Editions

Simon Walker (2008), *Leading with Everything to Give*, Piquant Editions

Margaret Wheatley (2001), From Hero to Host, intertview with Larry Spears and Roger Noble of Greenleaf, retreived from http://www.margaretwheatley.com/articles/herotohost.html

Index

CPSIA information can be obtained at www.ICGtesting.com
Printed in the USA
LVOW09s1208181014

409206LV00004BA/244/P